"I absolutely loved *God Has a Sound* by Lyndal J. Walker, our amazing Prayer Director at Youth for Christ! This book is a game-changer—an invitation to truly hear God in a world that's filled with distractions. Lyndal beautifully unpacks the many ways God speaks, from His gentle whispers to His mighty declarations, making it clear that His voice is the one we simply can't afford to miss. Reading this book felt like having coffee with a friend who reminds you to tune in to heaven's frequency. It's relevant for today—whether you're a seasoned believer or longing to hear God more clearly. The stories she tells are vibrant, relatable, and filled with wisdom. Lyndal, you are a gift to the body of Christ! Thank you for reminding us to listen to the sound that truly matters. I highly recommend this book—it's already transforming me, and I know it will do the same for you!"

Nthenya Macharia, Board Chair, Youth for Christ International

"I was captivated by the very first line and pulled into the text, page after page; Lyndal provides biblical evidence, historical realities and people's real experiences of the God who speaks, not just thousands of years ago but to this very day. If we are honest, what we really desire from our walk with God is to hear His voice. Lyndal helps us to find ways to turn down the noise of life and to become attentive to discovering how God is speaking directly to you and me."

Neil O'Boyle, National Director of British Youth for Christ

"My YFC colleague has penned a beautifully structured and illustrated book. It encourages us to grow in listening to God and worshipping Him, who loves us. This eye-catching book invites you and me to contribute an 11th chapter with our own story. Let's continue sharing these inspiring stories."

Edward de Kam, Senior Adviser for Youth for Christ Europe, Middle-East and North Africa

"Rich in biblical insights and personal illustrations, Lyndal J. Walker has authored a compelling guide that serves as a much-needed gift to the body of Christ. Anyone eager to deepen their friendship with Jesus, enhance their spiritual discernment, and learn how to listen to and interact with the voice of God will find this book a powerful and practical resource. *God Has a Sound* takes readers on an accessible journey through the experiences of various individuals: biblical authors, theologians, church leaders throughout history, and ordinary saints from around the globe, equipping them with the knowledge and tools necessary to enrich their experience of God. *God Has a Sound* also features stunning visuals that stir the imagination and help readers engage all their senses, enabling us to '*taste and see that the Lord is good.*' A must-read!"

Tim Horman, Senior Minister, One Church, Melbourne, Australia

"From the very beginning of this book, it's crystal clear that Lyndal is a passionate woman of prayer. She shares transformative ways to connect with God, offering compelling examples from the Word of God, international colleagues, and inspiring stories of historical figures known for their deep prayer lives. Get ready to be profoundly challenged and inspired!"

Karen Bott, Health and Resiliency Advisor, Youth for Christ Canada

"I'm so happy to have read this lovely little book. It's timely and very readable. Lyndal has done excellent research, and the inclusion of stories makes the content accessible to everyone. Our God is a 'speaking' God. While the Scriptures remain our anchor for truth, He desires to communicate with us humans in many varied ways, as Lyndal describes."

Fran Wylie, wife, mother, grandmother and teacher for Christian Academy, Ireland

God Has a Sound

Discovering the voice of God through the stories of His people

LYNDAL J WALKER

ARTWORK *by* KYLIE INGLIS

A Note on Quotations from the Bible

Sometimes different translations of the Bible give a different perspective on the Word of God.

Unless otherwise specified, all quotations are from the English Standard Version (ESV). Scripture quotations marked (ESV) are from The Holy Bible, English Standard Version ® (ESV ®), copyright © 2001 by Crossway, a publishing ministry of Good News Publishers. Used by permission. All rights reserved.

Other translations referenced are:

Scripture quotations marked (AMP) are taken from The Amplified ® Bible, Copyright © 1954, 1958, 1962, 1964, 1965, 1987, by the Lockman Foundation. Used by permission. (www.Lockman.org.) All rights reserved.

Scripture quotations marked (NASB) are taken from the New American Standard Bible ®, Copyright © 1960, 1962, 1963, 1968, 1971, 1972, 1973, 1975, 1977, 1995 by The Lockman Foundation. Used by permission.

Scripture quotations [marked NIV] taken from the Holy Bible, New International Version Anglicised Copyright © 1979, 1984, 2011 Biblica. Used by permission of Hodder & Stoughton Ltd, a Hachette UK company. All rights reserved. 'NIV' is a registered trademark of Biblica UK trademark number 1448790.

Scripture quotations marked (NKJV) are taken from the New King James Version ®. Copyright © 1982 by Thomas Nelson. Used by permission. All rights reserved.

Scripture quotations marked (NLT) are taken from the Holy Bible, New Living Translation, copyright © 1996, 2004, 2007, 2013 by Tyndale House Foundation. Used by permission of Tyndale House Publishers, Inc., Carol Stream, Illinois 60188. All rights reserved.

Written by Lyndal J. Walker

Artwork by Kylie Inglis

Cover Artwork: 'Shifting Shadows' by Kylie Inglis www.kylieinglis.com

Cover design and typesetting: Leysa Flores www.leysafloresdesign.com.au

Editing: inksnatcher.com

ISBN: 978-1-7365039-2-8

Published by: Youth for Christ International, Denver, Colorado. 2025.

To Warwick: Thank you for being an example of what it means to listen to and respond to God's voice. You listen well, brother.

Contents

Foreword		1
Introduction		7
CHAPTER 1	God speaks through creation	15
	Ember's Story — Confirmation in the clouds	21
	Highlight from History: George Washington Carver — Scientist	25
	Reflect	28
CHAPTER 2	God speaks through the Bible	31
	Sola's Story — The Scripture that changed an entire life	39
	Highlight from History: Martin Luther — A great reformer	44
	Reflect	46
CHAPTER 3	God speaks through dreams	49
	Lyndal's Story — Sceptic to believer	55
	Highlight from History: St. Patrick — Apostle to Ireland	59
	Reflect	61
CHAPTER 4	God speaks through visions	63
	John's Story — An early morning encounter	68
	Highlight from History: Perpetua — Mother and martyr	74
	Reflect	76
CHAPTER 5	God speaks through angels	79
	The Fulton's Story — A heavenly encouragement?	83
	Marcia's Story	85
	Highlight from History: The Waorani tribe of Ecuador	87
	Reflect	90

Chapter 6	God speaks through an audible voice	93
	Hilary's Story — The great escape	97
	Highlight from History: Florence Nightingale — Nurse, statistician and social reformer	101
	Reflect	104
Chapter 7	God speaks through people	107
	Vivienne's Story — Hearing God through art	111
	Highlight from History: William Wilberforce — Politician and social reformer	115
	Reflect	118
Chapter 8	God speaks through circumstances	121
	Matheus' and Muriel's Story — Divine alignment	125
	Highlight from History: John Wesley — Revivalist	129
	Reflect	132
Chapter 9	God speaks through the Spirit of Jesus/Holy Spirit	135
	Susan's Story — Heartbreak to hope	145
	Highlight from History: Jackie Pullinger — Missionary and founder of St Stephen's Society	149
	Reflect	152
Chapter 10	Postscript: Your Story	155
Acknowledgements		165
About the Author		167

Foreword

By Adam Shepski

As a disciple of Jesus, missionary, author and the executive director of Disciple a City (a growing ministry in Canada), I have an incredible need to hear the voice of God. Whether I am leading a ministry trip, preaching or building a national ministry, the joy of hearing God's voice has produced incredible fruit. As I have learned to obey Jesus through Bible reading and prayer, I have found surrounding myself with friends who hear God's voice an invaluable tool for my spiritual growth. Lyndal Walker is one of those dear friends.

I first met Lyndal at the beginning of 2015 at a Youth for Christ Australia staff conference, where I was the guest speaker while being part of the Youth for Christ Canada National Team. Before moving into Disciple a City full-time, I worked and travelled internationally to minister with Youth for Christ. This included travelling through an African desert

– on a near-broken bus – and dancing before the Lord in an Australian stadium, seeing thousands respond to Jesus. Lyndal is one of the most encouraging people I know. I have watched her lead youth, leaders and an entire organisation in prayer. Her faith and character are marked by humility, which has brought consistency to her leadership. This is why she has been entrusted with prayer leadership for the precious and effective ministry of Youth for Christ.

I was very excited when Lyndal told me she was writing a book about God's voice! All I know and appreciate about Lyndal is her love of Jesus and desire to help others hear His voice. The book you are about to read is written by someone who has prioritised her life around God's voice and direction. Lyndal lives the reality of what she writes, which gives her an incredible ability to communicate our need to hear God's sound.

I have heard the sound of God. I heard His voice just before a friend shared the gospel with me. I heard His voice at a prayer meeting when I first started attending church, and I heard His voice when I began reading the Bible. When I hear His voice, I have the opportunity to respond and obey; therefore, hearing God's voice has been the most transformative experience of my life.

The Bible is full of stories and examples of God speaking. This book shares the many varied ways God speaks through some of these stories and through historical and contemporary examples from people of faith around the world. When I study the Bible, I can easily conclude that God is still speaking today. Sadly, with all the incredible ways God has spoken to me, I am still far too unfamiliar with how He speaks. I long to hear every word and intention of His heart.

What I love about *God Has a Sound* is that Lyndal has prioritised the connection between hearing God's voice and Jesus's command to make disciples and fulfil the Great Commission. Her choice of chapters and stories honours her calling – and Youth for Christ's mission – to share the gospel with young people, no matter what! In chapter four, 'God Speaks through Visions', Lyndal shares the story of a young woman, Perpetua, who was martyred for her faith. Stories like hers give purpose to a vision from the Lord. It helped her endure intense persecution from the authorities of her time and allowed her to accept the outcome of persecution, a theme that is important for our own time in history and the reality of so many Christians, including YFC workers, around the world. As Perpetua's story highlights, we are called to expect that God will speak when we ask Him to.

I also love Kylie's artwork. These ethereal paintings add life and colour to the biblical narratives and helped me be fully immersed in the stories.

God Has a Sound has been more than another book for me. It has been an invitation to listen with my entire being. Lyndal's book, packed not just with stories but solid theology, has helped lead me to a fuller understanding of all the ways God speaks and left me hungry to hear Him more. Lyndal writes, 'God has a voice, and humans can hear it!' which challenged me to accept all the ways God speaks and ignited my faith to respond when He does.

Reading *God Has a Sound* will expand your understanding of how God speaks and give you faith to hear what He is saying to you. If you're like me, you want God to use your life. Lyndal's book will give you a framework to partner with God's voice and step into what God has called you to do. Savour each chapter and the stories within. Listen to what Jesus is saying, and you will find the direction, comfort and the provision you need to fulfil what He has called you to do.

Rev. Adam Shepski

Executive Director, Disciple a City

Missionary and author of *Untamed Obedience: How Simply Following Jesus Can Impact History*.

"Listen"

Introduction

God has a voice! And this voice has a sound. Do you know this? As one who has been in the practice of hearing God's voice for many years, I've known how He has spoken to me and others, but it wasn't until I was fasting and praying in February 2024, about a particular decision, that it became glaringly apparent that God has a sound. In the middle of the night, as I was tossing and turning from the turmoil of making this decision, I got out of bed to kneel and pray. I asked God what He wanted to say to me, and I was directed to Ezekiel chapter 10. As I began reading about Ezekiel's vision, verse 5 stood out.

'And the sound of the wings of the cherubim was heard even in the outer court, *like the voice of Almighty God when He speaks*' (Ezekiel 10:5 NKJV, my emphasis).

I didn't particularly know why I was directed to this chapter – it didn't seem to relate to what I was praying about – until that verse hit. You see, I had attempted to start this book in 2022 and had been making extremely slow progress due to a hectic 2023 with General Assembly[1] preparation. It was like

God was saying, 'Now is the time to get writing.' The decision was made, and I began writing in earnest.

Returning to the verse in Ezekiel, we can assume two things about God's voice when He speaks. Firstly, *God's voice is loud.* I don't know how far it is to the outer court from the entrance to the temple where the cherubim were (v. 3), but I assume it to be quite the distance[2] (if you're a Bible nerd, you can find out and let me know). This is what David, the shepherd King of Judah and Israel, says about the Lord's voice, as recorded in Psalms:

> *The voice of the Lord is on the waters;*
> The God of glory thunders,
> The Lord is over many waters.
> *The voice of the Lord is powerful,*
> *The voice of the Lord is majestic.*
> The voice of the Lord breaks the cedars;
> Yes, the Lord breaks the cedars of Lebanon in pieces …
> The voice of the Lord divides flames of fire.
> The voice of the Lord shakes the wilderness;
> The Lord shakes the wilderness of Kadesh.
> The voice of the Lord makes the deer give birth
> And strips the forests bare;
> And in His temple everything says, "Glory!"
> (Psalm 29:3–5, 7–9 NASB, my emphasis)

Wow, there are a lot of metaphors there, but what stands out is the noise and power! Ezekiel also uses the metaphor of God's voice sounding like 'many waters' when describing God's movement back into the temple in Jerusalem. In the

New Testament, John uses the terminology 'roar of many waters' when describing the voice of Jesus in heaven.

I've stood on the edge of Niagara Falls, on the border of Ontario, Canada and New York, USA, and I can tell you, these 'many waters' from four out of the five Great Lakes do roar! It is reported that the noise is between 87 and 95 decibels up close, about the same loudness as thunder![3] Isn't that interesting as David uses thunder in the same verse as 'over the waters'. Also, it isn't the only time David describes God's voice this way (see 2 Samuel 22:14 NASB). Job, that blameless man who feared God and was tested mightily by Satan, also described the thundering voice of God:

> Listen! Listen to the roar of his voice,
>   to the rumbling that comes from his mouth.
> He unleashes his lightning beneath the whole heaven
>   and sends it to the ends of the earth.
> After that comes the sound of his roar;
>   he thunders with his majestic voice.
> When his voice resounds,
>   he holds nothing back.
> God's voice thunders in marvellous ways;
>   he does great things beyond our understanding.
> (Job 37:2–5 NIV)

Even in the New Testament, when a voice came from heaven in response to Jesus praying, 'Father, glorify your name,' the crowd who heard it thought it had thundered. Only Jesus could hear the Father say, '"I have glorified it, and will glorify it again"' (John 12:28).

Secondly, from the verse in Ezekiel 10, we can assume that *God's voice can be known*. We can assume that Ezekiel had heard God's voice before because Ezekiel was able to describe that the sound of the wings of the Cherubim was *like* the voice of God. Of course, when we look back at the beginning of Ezekiel, we find that Ezekiel did indeed know the voice of God. In chapter 1, verse 24, he describes the sound of the wings of the living creatures as being 'like the noise of many waters, like the voice of the Almighty' (Ezekiel 1:24 **NKJV**), and when he sees the glory of the Lord, he falls on his face and he '*heard a voice of One speaking*' (v. 28, my emphasis). Chapter 2 and what follows tells of what the Lord spoke to him, which I won't expand on here. But do read it for yourself.

God has a voice, and humans can hear it! So why am I using stories in this book? What do stories have to do with God's powerful voice that can be heard? Because stories are a powerful means of communicating a message. We remember stories that have impacted us. In addition, there are three other significant reasons why stories are important, as pointed out by my local pastor[4]. Firstly, stories build community by highlighting commonalities, providing a sense of belonging, encouraging participation, sparking conversations, connecting with emotions, and fostering good relationships. Unity is a core value in Youth for Christ (YFC)[5], and as you read the stories of different YFC 'family members', I trust that you will see these things emerging within your own context. Secondly, stories build faith in the listener or, in this case, the reader. The stories selected here are a combination of both the miraculous and the very ordinary. Yet, all encourage greater faith in those willing to embrace the mark of the Divine. Thirdly, stories are a weapon. Revelation 12:11 says that our testimony is one of our tools against the devil. When we share stories of God's goodness, provision, faithfulness, love and, in this case, the way He has spoken (often in response to prayer), we counteract the lies the devil tells about us and God. The Enemy of our soul shudders at the stories of how God has spoken to His people because they are a means of advancing God's kingdom in this world.

From the very first pages of the Bible to its last, we discover that God has a voice and wants to be heard. From the creation of the world, where His voice made something out of nothing (Genesis 1:1–2), and His first words to humans, 'Be fruitful and multiply' (Genesis 1:28), to the culmination of the Lord's return in Revelation 22, where Jesus (who is God) says 'Behold, I am coming soon' (Revelation 22:7, 12, 20), the Bible is replete with stories of God speaking to us, His most precious of creations. All for the sake of us knowing Him and His ways. Through these stories, we discover that God can and does speak in various ways. But what does that mean for us today? Does God still speak in that loud, booming voice evident in the pages of the Scriptures? Can I hear God for myself? What might He sound like to me? By exploring some of these biblical stories and discovering how He has spoken to different historical figures and some of the YFC family, I hope you can start answering these questions yourself, and your hunger will grow to hear Him more clearly and follow Him more nearly[6].

In addition, I am delighted to have collaborated with the very talented Kylie Inglis, who has brought this book to life with her stunning artwork. These images are meant to be examined and prayerfully pondered as another means of God communicating to you (read about this in chapter 7).

May the sound of God penetrate your spirit as you read these stories and admire the beautiful artwork.

Lyndal J. Walker

Prayer Director, YFC International

Melbourne

INTRODUCTION 13

[1] General Assembly is a triennial conference run by Youth for Christ International for the global Youth for Christ family.

[2] From the research I've done, there is no certainty. Some say it could have stretched as far as 75 metres from the inner court. See https://www.swcs.com.au/tabernacle.htm#Temple (Accessed 13 February 2024).

[3] https://nyfalls.com/niagara-falls/faq-2/ para 10 (Accessed 12 March 2024).

[4] Notes from Darren Rowse, email 12 July 2024.

[5] Youth for Christ is an evangelistic organisation established in 1944 in the USA. It is now in around 133 nations with the aim of giving every young person in every people group in every nation the opportunity to make an informed decision to be a follower of Jesus and become part of the local church. For more information go to: https://yfci.org/about/

[6] 'Hear Him more clearly and follow Him more nearly are inspired by the lyrics of the DC Talk song 'Day by Day': https://www.google.com/search?q=Day+by+Day+lyrics+(DC+Talk)&oq=Day+by+Day+lyrics+(DC+Talk)&gs_lcrp

14 GOD HAS A SOUND

"They Opened Their Treasure Chests"

Chapter One

God speaks through creation

> In the beginning God created the heavens and the earth … And God saw all that He had made, and behold, it was very good.
> (Genesis 1:1 and 31 NASB)

> The heavens declare the glory of God;
>   the skies proclaim the work of his hands.
> Day after day they pour forth speech;
>   night after night they reveal knowledge.
> They have no speech, they use no words;
>   no sound is heard from them.
> Yet their voice goes out into all the earth,
>   their words to the ends of the world.
> (Psalm 19:1–4 NIV)

> Since the creation of the world God's invisible qualities – his eternal power and divine nature – have been clearly seen, being understood from what has been made, so that people are without excuse.
>
> (Romans 1:20 NIV)

'God, why haven't I experienced your glory the way Alex[7] has?' was my cry one night as I lay in bed, unable to sleep. The inner voice, becoming familiar to me, replied, 'Go outside and look up.' As it neared midnight, I dragged myself out of bed and stepped out of the side door. The night was dark, with no moon or streetlight in sight. As I emerged into this great darkness in the Australian bush and looked up, I realised why I had been invited to leave my bed and go outside. I looked up and stood in awe as the 100 billion stars of the Milky Way[8] cried out, 'The heavens declare the glory of God; the skies proclaim the work of his hands' (Psalm 19:1 NIV).

'You don't have to experience My glory like others have. My glory is all around you,' came the voice. Okay, I get it, God. My memory of that precious moment will never leave me. That night, God unequivocally spoke to me through His magnificent creation.

God's creation is very good. Do you believe that? In a world that is 'groaning' (see Romans 8:19–22) with myriad problems, our view of God's good creation can sometimes be obscured. Yet it is evident in God's Word that creation is one way He desires to speak to His people. Before a word was written in the Book[9], before a command was given to Moses, before David described what the voice of God was like, there was a blanket of stars and a luscious landscape shouting, 'Look how glorious the Creator is!'

A star like no other

After Jesus was born in Bethlehem in Judea, during the time of King Herod, Magi from the east came to Jerusalem and asked, 'Where is the one who has been born king of the Jews? We saw his star when it rose and have come to worship him.'

When King Herod heard this he was disturbed, and all Jerusalem with him. When he had called together all the people's chief priests and teachers of the law, he asked them where the Messiah was to be born. 'In Bethlehem in Judea,' they replied, 'for this is what the prophet has written:
'"But you, Bethlehem, in the land of Judah,
    are by no means least among the rulers of Judah;
for out of you will come a ruler
    who will shepherd my people Israel.'
Then Herod called the Magi secretly and found out from them the exact time the star had appeared. He sent them to Bethlehem and said, 'Go and search carefully for the child. As soon as you find him, report to me, so that I too may go and worship him.'
After they had heard the king, they went on their way, and the star they had seen when it rose went ahead of them until it stopped over the place where the child was. When they

saw the star, they were overjoyed. On coming to the house, they saw the child with his mother Mary, and they bowed down and worshipped him.
(Matthew 2:1–11a NIV)

When it comes to a biblical story of God speaking through His creation, we must dig deep. We don't necessarily have a straightforward biblical narrative to demonstrate this – unless you want to count God speaking through a donkey![10]

I have chosen the familiar story of the great star that led some pagan astrologers[11] to a newborn king. For those who are regular church attendees at Christmas, there is likely not a Christmas that goes by when this story is not retold. The narrative typically told goes something like this: three Magi, otherwise known as wise men, travel from a distant land in the East following a bright star to offer gifts of gold, frankincense and myrrh to a newborn king, who is the baby Jesus – sleeping snuggly in an animal feeding trough surrounded by sheep, goats, cows and His mum and dad, with possibly a shepherd or two thrown in. However, when we dig into this story, there is much to unpack, and this narrative is challenged. Firstly, we don't even know if there were three wise men, as it's not stated in the biblical story. Secondly, the fact that the story says it was a star doesn't necessarily mean it was one, as the Greek word here is a term used for a wide range of celestial bodies. Thirdly, with the timing of events in this story, we know that when the Magi arrived, Jesus was no longer a newborn but a toddler. Thus, the shepherds, whom the angels told to go and see the baby in a manger, were long gone[13].

Since the aim here is to reveal how God speaks through creation, I want to focus on the second point above: what part of God's creation did God use to 'speak' to these men from the East? I've read this story many times but only recently *really* noticed what it says in verse 2: 'Where is the one who has been born king of the Jews? We saw *his* star when it rose and have come to worship him' (my italics). It wasn't any old star, of which there are an estimated septillion (I didn't even know that was a number) in the universe[14]. It was '*his*' star'! How did these most likely pagan professional astrologers recognise and follow a star that led them to the Jewish Messiah?

It is important to note that in these ancient times, both Jews and Gentiles (non-Jews) believed that you could see signs in the heavens that pointed to significant events. Astrology was widespread throughout the Roman world, especially in the Near East, and astrology practitioners (astronomers of the times) were highly respected[15]. These ancient astrologers would have kept a close watch on the skies at a time when there were growing expectations of a Messianic king[16]. It is speculated that these astrologers were from Babylon, the ancient city where the Jews were exiled in the sixth century BC; therefore, they would have been familiar with the Jewish Scriptures and the prophetic insights the Scriptures gave[17].

While different scholars over the centuries have had various theories as to what the star was[18], modern tools used in astronomy mean that you can see exactly what was happening in the sky around the time that Jesus was born (which, by the way, is also debated) and thus what these ancient astrologers most likely saw to lead them to Bethlehem. Michael S. Heiser, a biblical scholar, said that in the year 3 BC, Regulus, the largest star in the constellation of Leo (the Lion), came into conjunction with Jupiter, the largest of the planets. Regulus was known as the 'king star' and Jupiter the 'king planet'. This would give the appearance of a massive star. In addition, Jupiter is known for its 'retrograde motion', its appearance moving back and forth in the sky. This happened a lot between 3 and 2 BC and can explain how 'the star went before them and rested over the place where the child was'. The Scriptures refer to Jesus as 'the Lion of the tribe of Judah' (Revelation 5:5). He is also called 'the King of kings' (1 Timothy 6:15, Revelation 17:14, Revelation 19:16). So, according to the proponents of this theory, Jesus was born on 11 September in 3 BC[19].

It is also interesting to note that Paul, in writing to the Romans, suggests that the stars (or the heavens) communicated the arrival of a divine King. In Romans chapter 10 and verse 18, he writes, 'But I ask, have they [Jews and Greeks, Romans 10:12] not heard [of Jesus, the Messiah]?' Indeed, they have, for 'Their voice has gone out to all the earth, and their words to the ends of the world.' (Romans 10:18)

What 'voice' is Paul referring to? He quotes Psalm 19:4 from the passage that begins with 'the heavens declare the glory of God'. Isn't it amazing that the God of the universe, who flung the stars into space (See Job 9:9, Psalm 8:3), aligned events in the heavens so that the people in the world at that time would be aware that the promised Messiah had arrived? I find it utterly stunning.

There are many details I'm skipping over here, so I highly recommend listening to the podcast referenced earlier, to get further insight. And even if you're an astrophysicist and have done all the research and believe a different conclusion, the point is that God, who created the stars and the planets, who had proclaimed through His Scriptures that a Messiah would come, arranged everything to line up at the exact moment in history for when this heavenly event would take place, and He used that to speak. It makes me stand in even more awe of our amazing God, and I hope it does the same for you.

Let's look at a more recent story of God using the heavens to speak. Ember is an American who has served with YFC in Botswana since 2010.

Ember's Story — Confirmation in the clouds

In 2006 I applied to join Youth for Christ as a missionary in Botswana. I was invited to attend the Candidacy School at the YFC headquarters in Colorado. The week involved training and fellowship, as well as psychological testing. We had to take a 566-question psychological examination and then discuss our results with a professional counsellor to ensure we were fit for the rigours of the mission field. Just after that week, the YFC leadership told me that I had been accepted, but they asked me to pray to be sure that YFC was the organisation with which God wanted me to serve.

Right afterwards, I was at my Minnesota church's fall (autumn) retreat in the north woods of Wisconsin. One evening I felt I should pray outside, looking up at the night sky. The thought came to mind several times during the evening: *Pray tonight, lying down, looking up at the sky.* So around 1 am, after everyone was in bed, I slipped out to head down to the dock on the lake. As I walked down there, I felt that perhaps this time of prayer would be when God would make it clear whether or not I was to join YFC. I was considering another organisation in Botswana, with which I'd served on a short-term trip in 2004.

I lay on the dock, looking up at the moon and the clouds drifting by. That's when a thought popped into my mind and caught me off guard: *What if God might use the clouds to spell something relating to His will?* I remember thinking how that would be testing God to ask for that – it would be a bit presumptuous. Would the God of the universe change the clouds just for *me?* But right after thinking that, I felt like God replied, *Yes, yes, I could and would do it just for you.* A rushing wind came, and I closed my eyes and bantered with God; *I'm not saying you couldn't! I believe you could do it if you wanted, I'm just not necessarily asking for it …*

I opened my eyes to see a very different scene of clouds than before I had closed them. What greeted my astonished eyes was a Y and a C in the clouds! The letters were not clouds but were empty spaces (dark, black sky) surrounded by lighter clouds, almost as if the Y and C had been drawn with a finger out of the backdrop of clouds. At first, my reaction was, *Wow … it's a Y and a C!* I was so new to Youth for Christ that it took me a second to realise that it looked like the logo, which is just a Y and a C (the F is an almost unnoticed extension of the Y). As the wind blew, the Y and the C converged in the middle, just like the YFC logo! I was so awestruck I couldn't say anything and headed back to the cabin to sleep.

As soon as I woke up, I wrote exactly what had happened and drew what I had seen. That day, Psalm 8 was the only psalm read in the church service:

> When I look at your heavens, the work of your fingers,
>   the moon and the stars, which you have set in place,
> what is man that you are mindful of him,
>   and the son of man that you care for him?
> (Psalm 8:3–4)

That could not have been more fitting. 'The work of your fingers'! And who am *I* that the God of the universe who created the heavens, the moon, and stars is mindful of me and cares enough for me to write in the clouds to confirm His will for me? Wow! I was just in awe and still am when I think about it.

I still find it hard to believe, so I expected some scepticism when sharing it. I only told my mentor, some missionary college classmates, and later a few close friends. When meeting with potential ministry partners over the following months, I would share how God had confirmed, over and over again, His calling on my life to Botswana. I would leave out the cloud story, though, because it wasn't needed to 'prove' my calling to Botswana. Honestly, in Western culture, it probably would decrease my credibility in some people's eyes, who might not believe that could happen. I assumed they might think, *Are you sure you passed that psychological examination …?*

However, one day in early 2007, the Lord shifted my perspective while driving from one meeting to another. I had just shared confirmation about my calling but left out the cloud part. The Lord spoke to my heart in the car: *If you're not sharing the cloud story, I'm not getting the glory for it.* Ouch! So, from that next appointment, I started sharing the cloud testimony more and found that it encouraged people to believe that God still does signs and wonders in the heavens today. It truly happened and is part of how God confirmed His will in my journey with Him, so I will share and allow Him to receive the glory.

Upon further reflection, I noticed an interesting connection. A few months before the cloud guidance, I had been praying and seeking God's direction on my next steps. I had graduated college and knew I was called to serve in Botswana, but I didn't know with which mission organisation (at that point, I didn't realise YFC was an option). While serving as a leader at my church's youth summer camp, the Lord assured me that He would clarify His guidance when needed. And where had He spoken that to me? Right beside that same lake in northern Wisconsin. The next time I was beside that lake a few months later, I'd say He made it pretty clear. Our God is truly an awesome God!

HIGHLIGHT *from* HISTORY

George Washington Carver — Scientist[20]

> I love to think of nature as an unlimited broadcasting station, through which God speaks to us every hour, if we will only tune in[21].
> George Washington Carver

Most Americans know him as 'the Peanut Man' — the man who came up with over 300 ways to use the peanut! However, George Washington Carver was first and foremost a man of faith with a deep love for nature, particularly flowers. He was born in 1864 to a slave woman in the state of Missouri, USA, at the time when the American Civil War was nearing its end. Southern raiders captured her and her newborn son (George) to sell to others, but their owner, Moses Carver, hired a scout to find them. There was no sign of the mother, but the baby was found alive, very sick, and Moses Carver repurchased him with a horse worth $300. This slave boy grew up on the Carver farm with no biological mother or father, but he and his brother were looked after like family by the Carvers, who were reluctant slave owners. As a boy, he had a curious mind and faith in God. He would spend hours in the woods collecting flower specimens and creating a secret garden. People from all around the area would bring him their sick plants, and he would nurture them back to health. He thus became known as 'the plant doctor'.

He desperately wanted an education; however, at the time, rural schools in the USA would not accept black people. When he was about thirteen, he collected a few necessary items and walked the eight miles (about thirteen kilometres) to a nearby town so he could go to school. He found shelter in a woodshed next to the school, and the owners of that shed ended up letting him stay.

After moving around to several different schools in the area, he finally graduated from high school at the age of twenty-one and went on to be the first black graduate of Iowa State College. He obtained a master's degree and became one of the greatest American scientists of the twentieth century.

One of his most outstanding achievements was saving the agricultural industry in the South. The heavy reliance on cotton crops depleted the soil, reducing yields. He advocated for and taught people how to do crop rotation with peanuts and sweet potatoes, which proved a great success. However, too much was produced, so he discovered hundreds of different uses for peanuts and sweet potatoes, which created a market for these crops. He also discovered 500 colour pigments that could be made from Alabama clay.

He credited all of this to his times of prayer with God. He regularly got up at 4 am to commune with God in the woods and get his daily instructions. He would go back to his laboratory, which he termed 'God's little workshop', to create his inventions:

> Here I talk to the little peanut, and it reveals its secrets to me. I lean upon the 29th verse of the first chapter of Genesis. 'And God said, Behold, I have given you every herb bearing seed which is upon the face of all the earth, and every tree in which is the fruit of a tree yielding seed; to you it shall be for meat.'
>
> What other materials do we need than that promise? Here I talk to the peanut and the sweet potato and the clays of the hills, and they talk back to me. Here great wonders are brought forth.[22]

You may very rightly ask the question, *How can these things talk back?* We need to read behind the words to the intent ... God was revealing and speaking His secrets through His creation for the benefit of others. As Psalm 25:14 says, 'The Lord confides in those who fear him; he makes his covenant known to them' (NIV).

Reflect

How about you? Have you ever had a moment where you stood in awe of God's creation and felt His still small voice whisper to you? Maybe it was on a dark, starry night, like me. Perhaps you saw a stunning sunset that is indelibly marked in your memory. Maybe you've talked to a bird as you've walked past on a country walk, and God's used it to speak back. Or you've looked up into the sky, and God's spoken in the clouds. May you slow down, take time out in creation and hear the sound of the Great Creator.

CHAPTER ONE   29

[7] Name changed.

[8] https://imagine.gsfc.nasa.gov/science/objects/milkyway1.html#:~:text=The%20Milky%20Way%20is%20a,in%20a%20really%20dark%20area (Accessed 13 March 2024).

[9] 'The Book' is a colloquialism for the Holy Bible.

[10] Read Numbers 22:22–35 for this fascinating story.

[11] See chapter 2 of *The Star That Astonished the World* by Ernest L. Martin, found at https://www.askelm.com/star/star002.htm (Accessed 13 March 2024).

[12] Heiser, M. (25 Dec 2016). Naked Bible Podcast, episode 138: What day was Jesus born? https://nakedbiblepodcast.com/podcast/naked-bible-138-what-day-was-jesus-born/ (Accessed 13 February 2024).

[13] For the story of the shepherds see Luke 2:8–21.

[14] https://science.nasa.gov/universe/stars/ (Accessed 20 May 2024).

[15] Molnar, M. R. (1999). *The Star of Bethlehem: The legacy of the Magi.* Rutgers University Press, New Jersey, p. 16.

[16] ibid. p. 8.

[17] See chapter 2 of *The Star That Astonished the World* by Ernest L. Martin, found at https://www.askelm.com/star/star002.htm (Accessed 20 May 2024).

[18] For some of these theories, see Molnar, M. R. (1999). *The Star of Bethlehem: The legacy of the Magi.* Rutgers University Press, New Jersey, chapter 2.

[19] Heiser M. (25 Dec 2016). Naked Bible Podcast, episode 138: What day was Jesus born? https://nakedbiblepodcast.com/podcast/naked-bible-138-what-day-was-jesus-born/ Also see https://bethlehemstar.com/ (Accessed 20 May 2024).

[20] The information contained here is from two sources: Clark, G. (1939). *The Man Who Talks with the Flowers.* Macalester Park Publishing Co. [St. Paul, MN], and the documentary by Ken Carpenter, *George Washington Carver: An Uncommon Way.* https://www.youtube.com/watch?v=49hizQFEssU (Accessed 12 April 2024).

[21] https://www.forbes.com/quotes/2257/ (Accessed 9 April 2024).

[22] Clark, G. (1939). *The Man Who Talks with the Flowers.* Macalester Park Publishing Co. [St. Paul, MN], p.17.

"Didn't Our Hearts Burn Within Us?"

Chapter Two

God speaks through the Bible

> All Scripture is breathed out by God and profitable for teaching, for reproof, for correction, and for training in righteousness, that the man of God may be complete, equipped for every good work.
> (2 Timothy 3:16–17)

Did you know the word 'bible' is not even in the Bible? The Bible (literally 'the book') is from the Greek *ta Biblia* (the books) and was taken over into Latin as a singular *Biblia*, 'the Bible', when Jerome translated it in AD 380[23]. It comprises sixty-six books, thirty-nine in the Old Testament and twenty-seven in the New Testament. When 'Scripture' or 'Scriptures' is read in the Bible, it refers to the Hebrew Bible, which includes *the Torah* comprising the five books of Moses (Genesis, Exodus, Leviticus Numbers, Deuteronomy), *the Prophets* (Joshua, Judges, Samuel, Kings, Isaiah, Jeremiah, Ezekiel and the Book of the Twelve prophets) and *the Writings* (Psalms, Proverbs, Job, Ruth, Lamentations, Ecclesiastes, Esther, Daniel, Ezra-Nehemiah, and Chronicles)[24]. These are the same books as in the Old Testament; however, Christians divide some of the books up, which accounts for the total of thirty-nine books[25].

The name 'New Testament' was first found in the writings of a theologian called Tertullian of Carthage in reference to the second part of the Christian Bible[26]. However, the books that should be included in this New Testament were not formalised until the late fourth century. If you want to learn more about how the Bible developed, I encourage you to read *The Canon of Scripture* by F. F. Bruce. The Bible, as it stands today, has been the primary way for people to hear from God throughout the last 1700 years or so.

A Scripture lesson like no other

> Now that same day two of them were going to a village called Emmaus, about seven miles from Jerusalem. They were talking with each other about everything that had happened. As they talked and discussed these things with each other, Jesus himself came up and walked along with them; but they were kept from recognising him.
> He asked them, 'What are you discussing together as you walk along?'
> They stood still, their faces downcast. One of them, named Cleopas, asked him, 'Are you the only one visiting Jerusalem who does not know the things that have happened there in these days?'
> 'What things?' he asked.
> 'About Jesus of Nazareth,' they replied. 'He was a prophet, powerful in word and deed before God and all the people.'
>
> (Luke 24:13-19 NIV)

He said to them, 'How foolish you are, and how slow to believe all that the prophets have spoken! Did not the Messiah have to suffer these things and then enter his glory?' And beginning with Moses and all the Prophets, he explained to them what was said in all the Scriptures concerning himself.

As they approached the village to which they were going, Jesus continued on as if he were going further. But they urged him strongly, 'Stay with us, for it is nearly evening; the day is almost over.' So he went in to stay with them.

When he was at the table with them, he took bread, gave thanks, broke it and began to give it to them. Then their eyes were opened and they recognised him, and he disappeared from their sight. They asked each other, 'Were not our hearts burning within us while he talked with us on the road and opened the Scriptures to us?'

(Luke 24:25–32 NIV)

Imagine the scene. You are with your friends in deep grief. The one you had hoped would save you from the power of the Romans had just been executed – a cruel, bloody crucifixion. Jerusalem is in chaos. Just a couple of days earlier, there had been a period of great darkness, a massive earthquake, and to top it all off, the great curtain in the temple (which separated the Holy Place from the Most Holy Place) had been split into two! And now, these women, who had been to His tomb with spices to prepare His body for proper burial, come barging in declaring that they'd seen angels who told them He's alive, that His body is no longer there!

It's all too much to take in. You need to get out of there. So you decide to take a walk with your friend. You can't help but recount all that's happened in the last few days, trying to make sense of it all. And then this stranger starts to walk with you and asks what's going on. He even dares to tell you you're a fool! He was obviously knowledgeable as he starts explaining everything from the Scriptures you hadn't put together yourself.

Obviously, at this stage, they didn't realise it was Jesus Himself who was explaining the Scriptures to them. But once their eyes were opened and they realised, they declared, 'Were not our hearts burning within us while he talked with us on the road and opened the Scriptures to us?' (Luke 24:32 NIV)

Have you ever thought about this? Jesus, the Creator of all things, used the Hebrew Bible to explain about Himself when He could have just easily said, 'Hey guys it's me!' He carefully went through what Moses had to say in the Torah and all the Prophets, interpreting the meaning as He went[29]. While we don't know the exact reason He used the Scriptures (perhaps He was modelling it so that they would also be able to use the Scriptures to share about Him with others), we do know that Jesus greatly valued the Scriptures for how God communicated to people through them as evidenced by the varying times He used the Scriptures in His teaching[30]. He also declared, 'Do not presume that I came to abolish the Law or the Prophets; I did not come to abolish, but to fulfill. For truly I say to you, until heaven and earth pass away, not the smallest letter or stroke of a letter shall pass from the Law, until all is accomplished' (Matthew 5:17–18 NASB).

As the story progresses, we find Cleopas and his friend back in Jerusalem, gathered together with the eleven disciples and others (Luke 24:33). As they explained to them what had happened, Jesus again showed up, this time revealing who He was from the beginning of the Scriptures (Luke 24:44-45).

One thing we can learn from Jesus's sharing with the disciples is that we often need an interpretation of the Scriptures, or an illumination of them, to understand what God might be saying to us. This could be from someone more mature in the faith or from the Holy Spirit Himself (See 1 Corinthians 2:6-16 and John 14:26). We see an example of this with Philip and the Ethiopian eunuch in Acts chapter 8 (Acts 8:26-39), where we find an Ethiopian reading from Isaiah. 'Philip asked, "Do you understand what you are reading?" The man replied, "How can I, unless someone instructs me?"' (Acts 8:30-31 NLT). Beginning from the Scripture that the eunuch was reading (Isaiah 53:7-8), Philip shared with him the good news of Jesus (Acts 8:35). As a result, the eunuch believed and was baptised (Acts 8:37-38).

The Bible has been used to justify all kinds of ungodly practices due to lack of correct interpretation, from Apartheid in South Africa[31] to the anti-semitism that led to millions of Jews being murdered by the Nazis[32]. While there is room for some differences in interpretation in the Christian faith[33], there are sound principles to use for interpreting Scripture. We call this *hermeneutics*. This includes considering the historical and cultural context (what was happening at the time), the type of literature a book is (for example, historical, poetic, a letter?), and if the language used is figurative or literal. One good book

I can recommend to help navigate the challenges faced in interpreting Scripture is *Slaves, Women & Homosexuals: Exploring the Hermeneutics of Cultural Analysis*[34]. Another to help with the different types of literature in the Bible is *How to Read the Bible for All It's Worth*[35].

I heard a sad story one time of a lady who cut off her hand due to the Scripture: 'And if your right hand is causing you to sin, cut it off …' (Matthew 5:30 NASB). This is an example of very poor hermeneutics. In this instance, Jesus uses this kind of language figuratively to make a strong point[36]. On the other hand (pardon the pun), many Scriptures have a plain interpretation, such as 1 Thessalonians 5:18 (NIV): 'Give thanks in all circumstances; for this is God's will for you in Christ Jesus'.

Whilst good hermeneutics is essential, it is also safe to say that God can speak through a singular Scripture or a series of Scriptures to speak to you personally and specifically. For example, as a young adult, the Lord started to talk to me about His heart for the poor and marginalised as I read varying Scriptures throughout the Bible about this. It was a theme that was repeated over and over that I could no longer ignore. This realisation was one crucial step in leading me to work alongside First Nation Australians for a season. Another example could be when you are struggling, and you randomly open the Bible to any page and point the finger, and it's precisely what you need to hear. God's love is so vast and so personal that He will use this means to speak to you even when you haven't put in the effort to understand the historical or cultural background of the Scripture. However, it is important to study diligently, too, especially if you are a worker in ministry. Paul's encouragement to a young Timothy was, 'Be diligent to present yourself approved to God, a worker who does not need to be ashamed, *rightly dividing the word of truth*' (2 Timothy 2:15 NKJV, my emphasis).

No one to explain, and yet …

Now, I want to turn your attention to an example of when the Holy Spirit brings illumination to the Scriptures to bring understanding. This story is from the early 1930s in outback Australia. Imagine you are five years old, playing with your sisters and cousins in a creek bed out in the bush, when suddenly, strangers come and take you away from everything you've ever known, all because of the colour of your skin. You are taken thousands of kilometres from your homeland, your mother and father and all you hold dear, to a strange building with strange beds and someone else to look after you. You do not know what they say because you speak a different language. And you are made to recite these strange words from a strange book repeatedly with absolutely no understanding of what you are saying. One day, you, your sister and your cousins go to the creek to mourn, wail and sing your people's songs. For some reason, you find yourself alone and in complete agony of grief for everything you have lost. As you watch the sunset over the hills, bawling your eyes out, a presence comes to you and interprets into your language the meaning of what you have been reciting but not understanding:

> I will lift up my eyes to the hills—
> From whence comes my help?
> My help *comes* from the Lord,
> Who made heaven and earth.
>
> He will not allow your foot to be moved;
> He who keeps you will not slumber.
> Behold, He who keeps Israel
> Shall neither slumber nor sleep.
>
> The Lord *is* your keeper;
> The Lord *is* your shade at your right hand.
> The sun shall not strike you by day,
> Nor the moon by night.
>
> The Lord shall preserve you from all evil;
> He shall preserve your soul.
> The Lord shall preserve your going out and your coming in
> From this time forth, and even forevermore.
> (Psalm 121 NKJV)

A great sense of peace comes over you, and you now understand that there is a God who will always watch over you no matter what might come. You can face another day with hope for better things to come[37].

It is a gift to have God's written Word and His presence through the Holy Spirit to help interpret. May we not take for granted this Book that is 'living and active, sharper than any two-edged sword' (Hebrews 4:12).

Let's now take a look at a story from a YFC leader in Africa.

Sola's Story — The Scripture that changed an entire life

I'm thankful to God for the person who discipled me when I became a Christian. One of the first things he taught me was to study my Bible and to study intentionally. He helped me understand that when I read my Bible, I can personalise the Scripture and hear God speaking to me through the pages.

He taught me that God gives commands from the Scripture, with instructions to follow and examples to learn from. We see examples of those who obey the command or instruction and those who don't obey or those who don't follow. From the examples, we see there is a reward for obedience. There's also a consequence for disobedience. So, you either get a blessing or a consequence. He also taught me that when I read my Bible, I should pause and ask the Holy Spirit to give me more insight when any word, phrase, or verse jumps out at me. One way to do this is by asking the 'now' questions: why, what, where, who, when, if – those six. I should always ask the Holy Spirit those questions. That became my pattern whenever I studied Scripture, and it helped me hear God speak.

For instance, I knew about the kind of woman I wanted to marry based on studying my Bible. As I read the story of Jacob, Rachel and Leah in Genesis 29, I realised that whoever I married had to be somebody passionate about the same thing I was passionate about in terms of calling or career. Jacob and Rachel were shepherds, so that became common ground for them. That helped me look out for the woman I wanted to marry as a young Christian.

Another instance was when I was struggling to decide whether or not to do full-time ministry with Youth for Christ. That day, I was studying Matthew 6, and I got to verse 33, which says, 'Seek first the kingdom of God and His righteousness, and every other thing shall be added to you.' He brought it up for me in economic terms. He said, 'Focus on the "end" (ministry) while I take care of the "means" (resources).'

One of the most compelling ways God spoke to me through Scripture was in 2010. I started sensing a kind of discontent or discomfort; I just started having this funny feeling that there was something new and a change coming. I needed to be sure of what exactly God wanted for me. During that period, our ministry expanded and was doing well in Lagos, as if I was at my peak. I didn't know what God wanted me to do: either a new ministry experience, maybe something new I needed to do, or a new approach to ministry. I wasn't sure exactly. I asked God, 'What exactly do you have in mind for me?' He directed me to go on a three-day retreat to seek Him out.

When I got there, I began by asking, 'So what next? What am I to do?' He directed me to the First book of John. I started reading from chapter one:

CHAPTER TWO 41

> That which was from the beginning, which we have heard, which we have seen with our eyes, which we have looked at and our hands have touched – this we proclaim concerning the Word of life. The life appeared; we have seen it and testify to it, and we proclaim to you the eternal life, which was with the Father and has appeared to us. We proclaim to you what we have seen and heard, so that you also may have fellowship with us. And our fellowship is with the Father and with his Son, Jesus Christ. We write this to make our joy complete.
> This is the message we have heard from him and declare to you: God is light; in him there is no darkness at all. If we claim to have fellowship with him and yet walk in the darkness, we lie and do not live out the truth. But if we walk in the light, as he is in the light, we have fellowship with one another, and the blood of Jesus, his Son, purifies us from all sin.
> (1 John 1:1–7 NIV)

As I read and studied this passage, He started clearly speaking to me: first, I was called to proclaim light to my generation, and second, I was a son of light. I felt that my life and everything about me were meant to reflect my calling, including my name.

My original family name, Famubo, meant 'the Oracle brought this child'. I had people tell me I needed to change it, but I didn't believe in changing names, so up until that point, I didn't. But the Holy Spirit told me, 'Sola, your name should reflect your calling.' God also reminded me of examples from the Bible of people whose names He had changed, such as Abram to Abraham, Jacob to Israel, and Saul to Paul, which gave me the confidence to change it. Then I asked God, 'What exactly am I to change my name to?' He said, 'Imoleolu', which means 'God's light'. The Holy Spirit said, 'You are God's light to your generation. So when your name bears that, that makes you conscious of My purpose in your life – for both you and your family.' That meant starting a new generation with me and my immediate family. Fortunately, my family didn't think I was crazy, and my wife and father were happy for me to change it since it was God's idea.

Beyond changing the name, He also gave me some other instructions from the first five to seven verses of this chapter, which changed my entire life, including that we should move to the North and start a mission agency, which was to reflect proclaiming Him as light to the people in darkness in those communities. That informed my resignation from Youth for Christ at that particular point in time in order to relocate. I didn't leave immediately; I gave the ministry enough time to transition to a new leader. We left about a year later once I got a replacement and had time to go to the new city to set up. I am now back working with YFC as the National Director of Nigeria and Regional Director of West Africa, but that is another story!

To sum up, if I sense the Holy Spirit speaking to me, I always clarify that instruction from Scripture. Scripture is the final authority on any leading that I have. If I get a leading that doesn't resonate with any Scripture, I check it out. I don't just jump into it; no matter how I feel the Holy Spirit is speaking to me. There must be a correlation with a Scripture from the Bible.

HIGHLIGHT *from* HISTORY

Martin Luther — A great reformer

The year was 1517. After much study of the Bible and great reflection, something had to be done. What was happening in the Church did not align with what was in the Scriptures. Selling indulgences[38] to poor people so they could have their sins forgiven was just the beginning. Martin Luther wanted to debate this, so he wrote down what is known as 'the 95 Theses' and nailed it to the Wittenberg Church door. What he wrote soon spread throughout Germany, and the Reformation was born.

Born in 1483 in Eisleben, Germany, Martin Luther became a monk in the Catholic Church after he survived a lightning bolt that struck near him as he was riding back to his university during a severe thunderstorm[39]. As a monk, he gave himself to 'prayer, fasting, and ascetic practices – going without sleep, enduring bone-chilling cold without a blanket, and flagellating himself'[40]. All this was done with the view of earning a place in heaven. He was made to study for his doctorate in the Bible and became a professor at Wittenberg University. He gave lectures on the Psalms and on Romans, and at some stage in his studies, he came to the realisation that righteousness (right standing with God) comes by having faith:

> I was seized with the conviction that I must understand [Paul's] letter to the Romans … but to that moment one phrase in chapter 1 stood in my way. I hated the idea, 'in it the righteousness of God is revealed.' … I hated the righteous God who punishes sinners … At last, meditating day and night and by the mercy of God, I … began to understand that the righteousness of God is that through which the righteous live by a gift of God, namely by faith. … Here I felt as if I were entirely born again and had entered paradise itself through gates that had been flung open.[41]

This realisation from reading and meditating on Romans transformed his life. Martin Luther went on to translate the Bible into German so that ordinary, everyday people had access to the Scriptures. Before that it was only the elite who could read the Bible as the Bible was only available in Latin in Germany[42]. Luther was not perfect and was known to be quite cantankerous, especially as he got older[43]. Despite his failings, he was a man greatly used by God to bring to light the truth of the Scriptures for everyday people and he changed the face of the West as a result.

Reflect

How about you? Are you a student of the Scriptures? Do you regularly take time out to study and hear from God through His Word? If not, what obstacles are in the way, and how can you overcome them? At no other time in history have we had greater access to the Bible through phone apps and audio translations. And just like Luther, translators worldwide are working hard to make it available in languages yet to be translated. We so often take for granted this way of God speaking. If we want to grow in hearing God, reading the Scriptures is a must. May we have ears to hear the sound of God through the Scriptures.

---

[23] Witherington, Ben (III). (2017). 'The Most Dangerous Thing Luther Did'. *Christianity Today*: https://www.christianitytoday.com/2017/10/most-dangerous-thing-luther-did/ (Accessed 9 April, 2024).

[24] F. F. Bruce. (1988). *The Canon of Scripture*. IVP, Downers Grove, p. 29.

[25] ibid. p. 29.

[26] ibid. p. 180.

[27] ibid. p. 232.

[28] Only the High Priest could enter the Most Holy place, once a year to atone for the sins of the people. See note on Luke 23:45 (NLT) in Life Application Study Bible, 3rd Edition, Tyndale House Publishers, Carol Stream (2020).

[29] Jesus could have used verses such as Genesis 3:15, Isaiah 53, Zechariah 12:10 and Malachi 3:1. For a fuller list, see *ESV Strong's* footnotes o and p on Luke 24:27.

[30] For example, in Luke 4 we see Jesus quoting from Isaiah 61:1–2 to begin his ministry. See also Matthew 7:12 'So in everything, do to others what you would have them do to you, for this sums up the Law and the Prophets' (NIV).

[31] Elelwani B. Farisani. (2014). 'Interpreting the Bible in the context of apartheid and beyond: An African perspective'. Studia Hist. Ecc. vol.40 n.2 Pretoria: http://www.scielo.org.za/scielo.php?script=sci_arttext&pid=S1017-04992014000300014#:~:text=The%20texts%20most%20frequently%20used,society%20and%20in%20the%20church (Accessed 1 April 2024).

[32] See: https://www.mdpi.com/2077-1444/9/1/26 (Accessed 14 February 2025).

[33] A couple of examples include whether women are allowed to teach in church when men are present or whether a person should be baptised as an infant or as a confessing adult.

[34] Webb, William J. (2001). *Slaves, Women & Homosexuals: Exploring the Hermeneutics of Cultural Analysis*. IVP Academic, Lisle.

[35] Fee, Gordan D. & Stuart, Douglas. (2014). *How to Read the Bible for All Its Worth* [Fourth Edition], Zondervan Academic, Grand Rapids.

[36] Stott, J. (Ed.) (1992). *The Message of the Sermon on the Mount (with Study Guide)*. The Bible Speaks Today Series, IVP, Leicester, p.89.

[37] This is the story of Mona Olsson, an Aboriginal Elder from Adelaide, South Australia. For her full story watch her interview at https://youtu.be/IgG1f4HCsbY (Accessed 14 February 2025).

[38] These were documents prepared by the church and bought by individuals either for themselves or on behalf of the dead that were said to release them from punishment due to their sins.

[39] https://en.wikipedia.org/wiki/Martin_Luther (Accessed 14 February 2025).

[40] https://www.christianitytoday.com/history/people/theologians/martin-luther.html (Accessed 4 March 2025).

[41] Kittleson, James M. (1992). 'The Breakthrough'. *Christianity Today/Christian History Magazine*. https://www.christianitytoday.com/1992/04/breakthrough/ (Accessed 4 March 2025).

[42] Witherington, Ben (III). (2017). 'The Most Dangerous Thing Luther Did'. *Christianity Today*: https://www.christianitytoday.com/2017/10/most-dangerous-thing-luther-did/ (Accessed 9 April 2024).

[43] https://www.christianitytoday.com/history/people/theologians/martin-luther.html (Accessed 9 April 2024).

"Here Comes The Dreamer"

Chapter Three

God speaks through dreams

> For God speaks again and again,
>   though people do not recognize it.
> He speaks in dreams, in visions of
> the night,
>   when deep sleep falls on people
>   as they lie in their beds.
> He whispers in their ears
>   and terrifies them with warnings.
> He makes them turn from
> doing wrong;
>   he keeps them from pride.
> He protects them from the grave,
>   from crossing over the river of death.
> (Job 33:14–18 NLT)

> "And it shall come to pass afterward,
>   that I will pour out my Spirit on all flesh;
> your sons and your daughters shall prophesy,
>   your old men shall dream dreams,
>   and your young men shall see visions.
> Even on the male and female servants
>   in those days I will pour out my Spirit.
> (Joel 2:28–29)

'Darwin 2009' were the words that came into my mind as I awoke in the middle of the night after a vivid dream. In the dream, I saw an outline of the map of Australia and a giant finger pointing at Darwin. It was the middle of 2007 and earlier that year I had travelled to Australia's 'top end' to volunteer at an Aboriginal school near this small, tropical Australian city. My heart had come alive with a calling and this dream, a few months later, brought confirmation, even though the timing was not what I would have wanted. My heart had already been captivated by the north and its people. But before I get into my story more, let's look at a 'dreamer' in the Bible.

Precocious teen to providential provider

One night Joseph had a dream, and when he told his brothers about it, they hated him more than ever. "Listen to this dream," he said. "We were out in the field, tying up

CHAPTER THREE 51

bundles of grain. Suddenly my bundle stood up, and your bundles all gathered around and bowed low before mine!"
His brothers responded, "So you think you will be our king, do you? Do you actually think you will reign over us?" And they hated him all the more because of his dreams and the way he talked about them.
Soon Joseph had another dream, and again he told his brothers about it. "Listen, I have had another dream," he said. "The sun, moon, and eleven stars bowed low before me!"
This time he told the dream to his father as well as to his brothers, but his father scolded him. "What kind of dream is that?" he asked. "Will your mother and I and your brothers actually come and bow to the ground before you?" But while his brothers were jealous of Joseph, his father wondered what the dreams meant.
(Genesis 37:5–11 NLT)

Joseph was Jacob's second youngest son, born to his second wife, Rachel (Genesis 35:24). He was a seventeen-year-old sometime shepherd who was a favourite child, whose dreaming got him into trouble with his brothers. He might not have been the wisest kid on the block, but what seventeen-year-old favourite child is? His dreams as a young man provoked his ten big brothers to such an extent that the hatred that they felt for him because he was favoured grew. When Jacob sent him to check on his brothers, who were watching the sheep, they plotted a scheme: 'They said to one another, "Here comes this dreamer. Come now, let us kill him and throw him into one of the pits.

Then we will say that a fierce animal has devoured him, and we will see what will become of his dreams'" (Genesis 37:19–20).

Fortunately, one of his brothers, Reuben, stepped in and told them not to kill him but just to throw him in a pit. He had a plan to rescue him later, but when a group of Midianite traders passed by, they decided to sell him to them, and they took him to Egypt. So, to cover up what they did, they smothered Joseph's unique coat of many colours with goat's blood to make it look like a wild animal had devoured him. This particular coat was given to him by his father as a sign of his special love for him, so you can imagine the devastation that Jacob felt when Joseph's brothers told him this lie (Genesis 37:12–36). The brothers thought that was the end of that … and those wretched dreams!

But, as Joseph's life unfolded in Egypt, despite all his hardships, he remained faithful to the Lord, and the Lord was with him (Genesis 39:2). He began to mature. When he was imprisoned for a crime he did not commit, his excellent attitude put him in good stead so that he was asked to look after two of the employees of the king of Egypt (the cupbearer and baker) when they were put in custody for an offence. They both had dreams one night, and they didn't know how to interpret them. Joseph's response was, 'Do not interpretations belong to God?' (Genesis 40:8) He then went on to successfully interpret them and asked to be remembered to Pharaoh that he might get out of there. But he was forgotten. It wasn't until two years later, when Pharaoh himself had a dream, that the cupbearer remembered Joseph and his successful interpretation of the dreams (Genesis 41).

Pharaoh summoned him to interpret this dream, and again, Joseph reiterated that it was not him, but God who could interpret. Once again, God gave him the interpretation and, as a result, Joseph went from the pit of a prison to a position of power when Pharaoh put him in charge over the land (Genesis 41:37). At this stage, he was thirty years old.

Yet the story continues. Pharaoh's dream was about a severe famine that would occur. Because of the forewarning, they could prepare during the good years, storing food for the lean years. When the lands around them began suffering, including Canaan, where Jacob and his sons lived, they came to Egypt for grain. And guess who happened to turn up! Yep, Jacob's brothers.

'Now Joseph was governor over the land. He was the one who sold to all the people of the land. And Joseph's brothers came and bowed themselves before him with their faces to the ground' (Genesis 42:6).

Of course, by this stage, Joseph was unrecognisable to them, and he wasn't about to make himself known to them. But he did remember the dreams he had as a youth. Eventually, after some testing of his brothers, he revealed his real identity. After around twenty-two years, there was a family reunion! Joseph declared, 'So it was not you who sent me here, but God' (Genesis 45:8).

God used dreams and dream interpretation greatly in Joseph's life to advance His purposes. While the fulfilment of those dreams that Joseph had as a seventeen-year-old was a long time coming, they were fulfilled in ways he would never have expected.

Of course, Joseph isn't the only dreamer in the Bible. God spoke many times through dreams to those who followed Him and to pagans who needed God's interpretation to understand them[44]. We see that some dreams God sent didn't need interpretation, like when He spoke to the other Joseph, Mary's husband, through an angel in a dream. In this dream, the angel said, 'Joseph, son of David, do not fear to take Mary as your wife, for that which is conceived in her is from the Holy Spirit' (Matthew 1:20). Whether a dream needs interpretation or not, it's important to remember, as Joseph and Daniel knew, that understanding came from God, and He needed to be enquired of to get it.

We are now in a time when the Spirit has been poured out. Peter declared the fulfilment of Joel's prophecy when the Holy Spirit came at Pentecost. If you have put your faith in Jesus for the forgiveness of sins and asked Him to be your Lord, you have the Spirit of God inside you. You, too, can be a recipient of God-given dreams. God has used dreams throughout history to speak to people and will continue to do so until His return.

Now I return to my own story.

Lyndal's Story — Sceptic to believer

I was a very sceptical young woman. I loved and wanted to obey God, but I had God in a box. I thought God only spoke through the Bible, and that was it. Of course, the Bible is the core of how we hear God's word. However, I missed the fact that the Bible was full of stories of God speaking supernaturally to people. It wasn't until I was in Bible college, throughout my mid to late twenties, that God showed me He couldn't be put in a box. There was a time when we were studying the Old Testament prophets, and I thought, *gee, I can relate to these guys*. While studying, I was also a youth and young adult leader at my church. Our youth pastors had a friend who was very much in tune with the voice of God and worked in a national youth ministry. They invited us youth leaders to spend some time with him, asking him questions about working with youth and how to help them grow as disciples of Jesus. The conversation centred around listening to them well and loving them no matter what. I remember questioning this and saying, 'But what if you feel like God wants you to say something to them to challenge them?'

His reply was not what I was expecting. 'Are you a prophet?'

With my stomach full of butterflies (nerves), I found myself saying, 'I think I might be, but I don't know what to do about it!' You see, I had no grid for the prophetic.

Let me clarify what I mean by 'prophet' and 'prophetic'. The definition of a prophet in the technical sense was a person who carried messages back and forth between humans and a god[45]. In the case of the people of Israel, this was Yahweh (the Lord). They operated on a national level, and often, the purpose was to call the people of Israel back to worship the one true God. In the Old Testament, the Holy Spirit would come upon people for these prophetic words and depart again[46]. When the Spirit of God was poured out at Pentecost, Peter saw it as the fulfilment of Joel's prophecy that one day, the Spirit would be poured out on all people, and they would prophesy (Acts 2:17–18). This gift is now available to all who have put their faith in Jesus and have God's indwelling Spirit. Paul lists it as a gift of the Spirit (1 Corinthians 12:10), however, now it is not for the nation of Israel but for the building up and encouragement of the body of Christ (1 Corinthians 13:1–5). When I said I thought I might be a prophet, it was in the sense of one with the gift of prophecy, something I hadn't been taught about before. I have since learned that a prophet in the New Testament sense works alongside apostles, evangelists, shepherds (pastors) and teachers to equip God's people for works of service and to mature them in Christ (Ephesians 4:11–16).

That night, my newfound friend and my fellow youth leaders affirmed me, and he prayed a prayer of blessing over me, acknowledging that gift in my life. For the next three nights in a row, I had such vivid dreams as I had never had before. After the third night, God had my attention. I knelt and cried out, 'I know you spoke to people in the Bible through dreams, so if you're trying to speak to me, you better show me what these dreams are about.' As soon as I prayed that prayer, I started

CHAPTER THREE 57

getting ideas coming to my mind of what these dreams were indeed about. This began a journey of really seeking after God and learning all I could about the voice of God. This man ended up becoming a mentor and I would ask him many questions, but he would always point me back to Jesus to find out what He was saying, which was the best advice he could give! Twenty-plus years later, he is still a huge encouragement to me and is part of my prayer support team.

It has been an exciting journey since. I have received dreams for myself for guidance or simple encouragement, to bring encouragement or gentle correction to others, and even to bring insight into situations in church or ministries. Is every dream from God? Certainly not, but the ones that stick out are the ones you need to pay attention to. Of course, the Enemy can also send dreams, in the form of nightmares or other deceptions, and I've also had my share of them. Whenever you think a dream has a message from God, you need to make sure it aligns with God's heart and character and is in line with His written word. If a person might give accurate information in a dream but then tries to lead you away from the one true God, they must not be listened to. This is what Moses had to say about that:

> If a prophet or a dreamer of dreams arises among you and gives you a sign or a wonder, and the sign or wonder that he tells you comes to pass, and if he says, "Let us go after other gods," which you have not known, "and let us serve them," you shall not listen to the words of that prophet or that dreamer of dreams. For the Lord your God is testing you, to

know whether you love the Lord your God with all your heart and with all your soul. You shall walk after the Lord your God and fear him and keep his commandments and obey his voice, and you shall serve him and hold fast to him.
(Deuteronomy 13:1–4)

The punishment of one who would lead such a rebellion against God was severe – death! (Deuteronomy 13:5)

We can assume it's both your and my intention not to turn people away from the one true God, so I think we're pretty safe there. We operate through the lens of the New Covenant God gave through His son, a covenant of love and grace[47]. In seeking the Lord about our dreams, we may be off the mark at times, but if there is something He really wants to communicate to us, He certainly is big enough to bring confirmation through other means[48].

I do not intend to teach the topic of dreams and their interpretation in depth here. Other people have done that. I encourage you, if this is a journey you are on yourself and are hungry to learn more, read extensively, firstly from the Bible (Daniel is one of my favourite books of the Bible for learning about God speaking through dreams and interpreting them) and secondly from others such as Jack Deere's *Surprised by the Voice of God*[49] and Thompson & Beale's *The Divinity Code to Understanding Your Dreams and Visions*[50].

HIGHLIGHT *from* HISTORY

St. Patrick[51] — Apostle to Ireland

Seventeenth March – do you know what is celebrated on this day? It is St Patrick's Day, the national day of Ireland. Many people worldwide celebrate this day by dressing up in green, attending parties and parades and going to the pub for a pint of Guinness. I wonder what the man himself would have thought about this? Patrick was known as 'the apostle to Ireland' and was key in bringing Christianity to the then-pagan Irish people. And he wasn't even Irish!

Patrick was a Roman Britain born in AD 385. He was likely from a Christian family, although he did not consider himself religious as a young person. It wasn't until he was captured by Irish raiders and taken to Ireland as a slave that he began a personal relationship with God. He was sixteen years old with no surviving immediate family members, as they had all been slaughtered in the raid. He most likely watched his parents die.

For six years, he was left outside to watch the sheep and cattle in the harsh Irish landscape and the even harsher winters of wind, ice and snow. It was in this environment that he encountered the love of God. God so enamoured him that he would get up at dawn to pray and spend many hours in prayer and fasting. It was in this environment that Patrick started dreaming dreams. He records that one night, he dreamt of an angel figure called Victor who said, 'You have done well in your fasting. Soon, you will go back to your homeland.' A couple of nights later, he was again disturbed by another dream in which Victor appeared and told him, 'Your ship is ready.' The very next day, he decided to run away – a dangerous thing for an enslaved person to do. He walked over two hundred miles to the southeast of Ireland before finding a ship. The sailors agreed to take him on board, but they ended up shipwrecked in France. Starving, the pagan sailors prayed to their gods, but nothing happened. They asked Patrick to pray to his 'Christian God', so he did, and a herd of pigs appeared! They were thus saved from starvation and eventually returned to Britain.

After being reunited with some extended family members, they begged him never to go anywhere because of the terrible things he'd been through. However, God spoke to him in another dream. This time, a man called Victoricus appeared with innumerable letters from people calling to Patrick to 'come walk once more among us'[52]. He woke up feeling heartbroken. He decided to get training in France and become a priest. After a couple of decades, he returned to Ireland, the place of his captivity, to bring the gospel to the Irish people. He is known as one of the most successful evangelists in history.

Reflect

How about you? Have you ever had a dream that made you sit up, take notice, and think that God was speaking to you through it? How do you think you would react if God did give you a dream? Would your theology say, 'That can't be God'? Like me, I encourage you to take God 'out of the box' and begin to listen to this sound of God.

---

[44] For example, Nebuchadnezzar as told in Daniel 1 and 2.

[45] 'Prophet', *Eerdman's Dictionary of the Bible* by David Noel Freedman (ed.) (Accessed from Olive Tree App).

[46] For examples see 2 Chronicles 15, 2 Chronicles 24:20, 1 Samuel 10:9–10.

[47] For some texts on the new covenant see Jeremiah 31:31–4, Hebrews 8–9, 2 Corinthians 3:6, Matthew 26:28, Romans 7:6, John 13:34.

[48] See the story 'An unforgettable lesson' as an example of this in Deere, J. (1996). *Surprised by the Voice of God: How God Speaks Today Through Prophecies, Dreams, and Visions*. Zondervan, Grand Rapids, MI, pp. 229–232.

[49] Deere, J. (1996). Surprised by the Voice of God: How God Speaks Today Through Prophecies, Dreams, and Visions. Zondervan, Grand Rapids, MI.

[50] Thompson, A. F. & Beale, A. (2013). *The Divinity Code to Understanding Your Dreams and Visions*. Destiny Image, Shippensburg, PA.

[51] The information here is summarised from the documentary *St Patrick: Pilgrimage to Peace*, by Global Story Films: https://www.youtube.com/watch?v=utv-QzQBZlE (Accessed from YouTube, 21 March 2024).

[52] See Acts 16:9 which tells of a dream that Paul had where a man from Macedonia appeared urging him to 'Come over to Macedonia and help us'.

"The Way"

Chapter Four

God speaks through visions

When I typed 'vision' into my ESV *Strong's Bible*[53], it came up with eighty-nine hits! Across both the Old and New Testaments, we see the records of God speaking to His people through visions. So, what is a vision? In the English language sense, we could say that it is a visual (something seen) or auditory (something heard) event that reveals something otherwise unknown[54] ... most likely when a person is awake (it's a dream when a person is asleep). *The Dictionary of Jesus and the Gospels* states that the ancients saw dreams and visions as more fluid, often using the same terminology for both[55].

Self-righteous persecutor to powerful apostle

But Saul, still breathing threats and murder against the disciples of the Lord, went to the high priest and asked him for letters to the synagogues at Damascus, so that if he found any belonging to the Way, men or women, he might bring them bound to Jerusalem. Now as he went on his way, he approached Damascus, and suddenly a light from heaven shone around him. And falling to the ground, he heard a voice saying to him, "Saul, Saul, why are you persecuting me?" And he said, "Who are you, Lord?" And he said, "I am Jesus, whom you are persecuting. But rise and enter the city, and you will be told what you are to do." The men who were traveling with him stood speechless, hearing the voice but seeing no one. Saul rose from the ground, and although his eyes were opened, he saw nothing. So they led him by the hand and brought him into Damascus.
Now there was a disciple at Damascus named Ananias. The Lord said to him in a vision, "Ananias." And he said, "Here I am, Lord." And the Lord said to him, "Rise and go to the street called Straight, and at the house of Judas look for a man of Tarsus named Saul, for behold, he is praying, and he has seen in a vision a man named Ananias come in and lay his hands on him so that he might regain his sight."
(Acts 9:1–8, 10-12)

I could have chosen great visionaries such as Ezekiel, Isaiah, or John, whose visions are recorded in detail, to highlight here. So why did I choose the story of Saul (renamed Paul) instead? Visions played a significant role in his conversion story and, consequently, how much impact this man has had on the Church through the ages. After all, thirteen of the twenty-seven books of the New Testament are attributed to Paul[56].

Saul, a learned Pharisee and a persecutor of the followers of Jesus (Acts 8:1–3), was on a mission from Jerusalem to Damascus[57] to find more of these followers to capture and imprison. After trekking across the countryside with murderous threats in his heart, he was just about at his destination in the bright noonday sun (Acts 22:6) when an even brighter, heavenly light appeared. Did Jesus appear in person? Well, we can't know for sure, but Paul did say that the men travelling with him heard the voice but saw no one, which indicates that Paul probably did see Jesus in real life. However, in recounting this experience when giving his defence to King Agrippa, Paul described it as a heavenly vision in which he heard Jesus speak (Acts 26:19). As the story continues, Ananias, a disciple of Jesus residing in Damascus, also had a vision where Jesus told him to go and heal Saul of the blindness caused by the heavenly encounter. With some apprehension (because of the stories of persecution he had heard), Ananias obeyed the Lord. I don't know about you, but I think I would need the clarity of a vision to go to speak to a known terrorist!

The Lord prepared Saul for Ananias's arrival by giving him another vision ... he could 'see' even though he was blind. After spending some time with Ananias and the other disciples in Damascus, Saul returned to Jerusalem and prayed in the temple when he 'fell into a trance' (Acts 22:17–18). In the trance, Jesus warns him to get out of Jerusalem quickly 'because they will not accept your testimony about me' (Acts 22:18). In the same trance, the Lord gives him his calling, saying, 'Go, for I will send you far away to the Gentiles' (Acts 22:21).

What is the difference between a trance and a vision? Trance ('ekstasis' in the New Testament Greek[58]) is the state of mind where everything in the material world fades, and the mind is solely fixed on what is seen in the subjective. It is the state of mind where a person can receive a vision. It sounds like something out of the New Age, doesn't it? When we are discussing things of the supernatural, we must be aware that Satan is a counterfeiter. He has no original ideas and only takes what God created as good and twists it for his evil means. Even though Paul had these supernatural experiences, in 2 Corinthians 11:14, he warns us that 'even Satan disguises himself as an angel of light.'

As for the instances when God speaks through dreams, we must be sure that whatever we believe God might be saying in a vision aligns with what is written in the Word of God. The Word of God is the final say in all matters, so if the vision is leading us away from what we know to be true from the Bible, we must realise that deception from the Enemy is involved. Both the Old and New Testaments warn of false visions and false prophets:

> The word of the Lord came to me: "Son of man, prophesy against the prophets of Israel, who are prophesying, and say to those who prophesy from their own hearts: 'Hear the word of the Lord!' Thus says the Lord God, Woe to the foolish prophets who follow their own spirit, and have seen nothing! Your prophets have been like jackals among ruins, O Israel. You have not gone up into the breaches, or built up a wall for the house of Israel, that it might stand in battle in the day of the Lord. They have seen false visions and lying divinations. They say, 'Declares the Lord,' when the Lord has not sent them, and yet they expect him to fulfill their word. Have you not seen a false vision and uttered a lying divination, whenever you have said, 'Declares the Lord,' although I have not spoken?" Therefore thus says the Lord God: "Because you have uttered falsehood and seen lying visions, therefore behold, I am against you, declares the Lord God. My hand will be against the prophets who see false visions and who give lying divinations. They shall not be in the council of my people, nor be enrolled in the register of the house of Israel, nor shall they enter the land of Israel. And you shall know that I am the Lord God."
> (Ezekiel 13:1–9)

> Beware of false prophets, who come to you in sheep's clothing but inwardly are ravenous wolves. You will recognise them by their fruits.
> (Matthew 7:15–16)

> Beloved, do not believe every spirit, but test the spirits to see whether they are from God, for many false prophets have gone out into the world.
> (1 John 4:1)

Paul continued having visions throughout his life. In his letter to the Corinthian church, he recounts one of these visions in the third person (2 Corinthians 12:1–7). He said these revelations were so great that he was given a 'thorn in his flesh, a messenger from Satan' to keep him from becoming conceited (2 Corinthians 12:7).

While not everyone will receive extraordinary visions and revelations as Paul did, the Lord still uses visions to communicate with His people today.

John's[59] Story — An early morning encounter

I was born in a former Soviet Union state. My country left the Soviet Union at the end of 1991 and a Civil War broke out in 1992. I was just 19 years old. Everything had changed, not only for me but also for many people in my life.

Of course, as a young person, I also experienced a crisis at this time. I didn't know how to move forward or what my future held. At that time a missionary came from the USA and started a church. I liked a girl in leadership at this church very much, so I started going along because of her. This led me to become a member of the church.

Unfortunately for me, that girl married a missionary after a while, and they left the church and my country. So I thought, *Well, why should I bother continuing to go to the church? She's gone. So why do I do that now?'*

However, I noticed that people who attended experienced God differently, and their lives started to change. I couldn't understand what was going on or what power influenced their lives that I didn't have.

When I was still in love with that girl, I thought I would start dating her and then get her out of that strange environment. But then one of my friends said, 'You know, there really is a God, and you can actually have this experience of encountering Him.'

At that point in my life, I said a straightforward prayer: 'God, if you exist, if you are there, please meet with me or let me know.'

When I said that prayer, I had been attending church for a year and a half. But I couldn't say I had faith because my only reason for going was to meet the girl I liked. I can definitely say that you can attend church but not have faith in God. By then, I had learned how to behave in church. I knew all the songs, when to sit down and stand up, and all the rituals and routines.

I was okay with all this, but I had no personal connection or relationship with the Lord.

In November of 1993, I went with a small group from the church to a neighbouring country to attend a Christian conference. I was feeling the load of disappointment. *What is the sense of all this? What am I doing here?* These were the questions that plagued me. In the early morning of 24 November, at about 5 am, I suddenly felt unsettled, like something in my heart was disturbed. With this feeling of unrest, I walked outside and thought, *okay, God, where are you?* Right then, in the early morning, I heard a clear voice: 'John, I am here.'

I started looking around as if somebody was talking to me. Then I thought, if it is God, I must look up to the heavens (sky) to see Him. I could see a wide cloud in the sky, and the clouds were moving, but then suddenly, they stopped and formed something like a circle above my head. That definitely drew my attention.

I started to look at those clouds, and immediately, the clouds, which were in the shape of a circle, very quickly took the shape of a person. It was as if a person, wearing a long robe, standing full size with outstretched hands, wanted to embrace me. I stood astonished, and then I heard the voice speaking again, saying, 'This is me. Jesus.'

I squeezed my eyes closed, and I was like, 'No, no, no! That can't be true!' – like I might be going crazy. I thought if I spent some time with my eyes closed, then this image would disappear, and everything would go back to normal, but when I opened my eyes again, it was still there!

It hit me deeply. If this is God, then right now, He must be looking at me. I felt like a tiny person, like a small insect, and this big God was looking at me right now. It felt like I had encountered Him face to face.

I knew that I needed to somehow respond at that moment and say something to God. I said, 'Lord, if it is you, I submit everything I have in my life into your hands.'

God replied, 'I don't need your things or your life. I own everything that exists. I just want you to follow me.'

When I heard that, I felt profound freedom, life, and hope for the future. Before that, it was like I was imprisoned, but God set me free. I felt as if I could fly!

The next feeling I had was as if I was jumping from the edge of a cliff down to the ocean, and this ocean was the love of God where I would dive in and swim.

So, as I stood there before the Lord, I said, 'Yes, Lord. I will follow you.' After I said this, the image of Jesus disappeared.

But there were still some things God wanted to say to me. He first said that as long as I preached, I would remain alive, and my life would be spared. This message was important to hear from the beginning of my walk with Him. As I look back on the past thirty years of my life, I can see His intervention when there were direct threats to my life. In these situations of danger, as I continued to preach, the circumstances would change, and I remained alive. For example, once, a gang of forty criminals surrounded me, and they intended to kill me. But as I started preaching, they stopped attacking, and their leader suddenly protected me. The whole situation just changed its course, and they brought me to a safe place. There were many more dangerous and life-threatening situations I found myself in, but when I preached to the people who wanted to kill me, people would repent, and I would be saved. The most extreme was when I was an assistant pastor. A bomb was planted underneath the seat that I usually sit in at church every Sunday. However, I was preaching on the stage that Sunday, so my life was spared. Sadly, others were killed that day.

The second thing God said early in the morning on that day was that I should preach about this experience I had with Him. I have had the opportunity to share this story at a Mosque, with military personnel, government ministers, famous actors and actresses, and all kinds of people.

The third thing God said was that I would preach worldwide (even though I don't speak English). And that has come to pass. I have had the opportunity to speak in many countries without knowing the language or culture.

The last thing God said to me that morning was, 'Remember the promise you have made to me today.'

I didn't want to tell anyone about my encounter that morning. All day, I kept it to myself. That night was the beginning of the conference. I took my seat at the back of the room. The speaker from the USA got up on the stage and said, 'Before I start my message, I want to share a miracle I saw today. At 5 am this morning, I saw Jesus in the clouds.' Wow! This person I didn't know from the other side of the world had seen what I had seen! God used this to confirm that this encounter had happened and not to doubt what I had experienced. I needed this for the future moments in my life when I would doubt and fear. Every time I started to doubt or fear, I would remember my encounter with Him that early morning in 1993.

All of this is not about me, but it's about the God who met with me in such an amazing way thirty years ago.

HIGHLIGHT *from* HISTORY

Perpetua — Mother and martyr

The year is AD 203. The stage is set for 'the games' in Carthage, North Africa. The amphitheatre is full of Romans of varying classes, ready to celebrate the emperor's son's birthday by watching the gladiators and convicted criminals fight to their deaths[60]. Among these 'criminals' are Christians, including the young mother Perpetua. Well-educated and from a prosperous family, twenty-two years of age and still with her child needing to be breastfed, she was a catechumen (a convert not yet baptised)[61]. Perpetua was a woman of remarkable faith who kept a journal while in prison, the oldest surviving writing by a Christian woman.

The wild beasts would have their way with these Christians, arrested and sentenced to death for their allegiance to Christ. But Perpetua already knew that. While imprisoned in a Roman dungeon, she asked the Lord for a vision:

> I made my request, and this was the vision I had. ... I saw a ladder of tremendous height made of bronze, reaching all the way to the heavens, but it was so narrow that only one

person could climb up at a time. To the sides of the ladder were attached all sorts of iron weapons ... At the foot of the ladder lay a dragon of enormous size, and it would attack those who tried to climb up and try to terrify them from doing so.[63]

She describes stepping on the dragon's head to climb the ladder and being greeted by a grey-haired shepherd in a garden, who is accompanied by thousands of people in white garments.

In another vision, she was led to the centre of the arena by Pomponius (a deacon), where she was to battle with an Egyptian. She states, 'In the vision, I knew that I was condemned to die by the beasts.' The vision goes on to describe the battle and One who was with her in the struggle, like a trainer and assistant to help her. In the end, she defeated the Egyptian by stepping on his head. The trainer kissed her and said, 'Peace be with you, my daughter.' She began to walk in triumph towards the Gate of Life[64].

Her writings include a couple of other visions, which I won't consider here. The Lord used these to help prepare her to face the arena with courage, knowing that her death would end in eternal triumph.

Stories like this are not often the ones we want to read about as, in the earthly sense, there is no happy ending. Yet the pages of history are full of faithful followers of Jesus who met their untimely demise through cruel means (just read Hebrews chapter 11 as an example). However, we know that from a heavenly perspective, there is a great reward for those who are faithful amid such harsh persecution (James 1:12, Revelation 2:10).

Reflect

How about you? Are you ready to stand for Jesus no matter the cost? Have you ever asked God to give you a vision for your future? You don't have to be in a literal dungeon, but perhaps you are going through an earthly trial that is severely testing your faith. What would God want to speak to you about that today? May we have ears to hear and eyes to see the sound of God in this way.

[53] The Olive Tree Bible App.

[54] 'Vision'. *Eerdman's Dictionary of the Bible* by David Noel Freedman (ed.). (Accessed from Olive Tree App).

[55] 'Dreams and Visions'. *Dictionary of Jesus and the Gospels*, Joel B. Green. (Accessed from Olive Tree Bible App).

[56] 'Paul'. *Eerdman's Dictionary of the Bible* by David Noel Freedman (ed.). (Accessed from the Olive Tree App).

[57] A distance of about 135 miles or 218 kilometres.

[58] *Olive Tree Enhanced Strong's Dictionary*, g1611.

[59] Name has been changed.

[60] Kreider, A. (2016). *The Patient Ferment of the Early Church*, Baker Academic, Grand Rapids, p. 40.

[61] 'Catechumen'. *Oxford Languages Dictionary* (Accessed 17 July 2024).

[62] Franciscanmedia.org: https://www.franciscanmedia.org/saint-of-the-day/saints-perpetua-and-felicity/#google_vignette (Accessed 26 March 2024).

[63] Joyce E Salisbury. (1997). *Perpetua's Passion: The Death and Memory of a Young Roman Woman*. Routledge, London, p. 99–100.

[64] ibid. p. 108.

"... (Because You Did Not) Believe My Words..."

Chapter Five

God speaks through angels

'You have a big angel standing over you,' said my friend as we got ready for church that morning. I didn't feel or see anything, yet my friend could see with her spiritual eyes to reassure and comfort me. Our church had been going through quite a spiritual battle during the preceding weeks, and I had been interceding, asking God for a breakthrough. We were hoping to discern what God wanted us to do that morning. Ultimately, things at our church didn't work out as I would have liked, and there was a church split. While it was a very painful time for many people, myself included, the Lord used this time to show us how real the spiritual realm is, and that there are real spiritual beings at work today, not just in the pages of Scripture or old stories. While I've never had an angel appear or speak to me, Scripture is full of stories of people who heard from these God-sent messengers. Let's take a look at one such story.

An announcement that left a man speechless

In the days of Herod, king of Judea, there was a priest named Zechariah of the division of Abijah. And he had a wife from the daughters of Aaron, and her name was Elizabeth. And they were both righteous before God, walking blamelessly in all the commandments and statutes of the Lord. But they had no child, because Elizabeth was barren, and both were advanced in years.

Now while he was serving as priest before God when his division was on duty, according to the custom of the priesthood, he was chosen by lot to enter the temple of the Lord and burn incense. And the whole multitude of the people were praying outside at the hour of incense. And there appeared to him an angel of the Lord standing on the right side of the altar of incense. And Zechariah was troubled when he saw him, and fear fell upon him. But the angel said to him, 'Do not be afraid, Zechariah, for your prayer has been heard, and your wife Elizabeth will bear you a son, and you shall call his name John.' ... And the angel answered him, 'I am Gabriel. I stand in the presence of God, and I was sent to speak to you and to bring you this good news.'

(Luke 1:5–13, 19)

This story is probably familiar if you have been a Christian for a while. Still, perhaps you have bypassed it on the way to another famous Gabriel story that is usually recounted every year at Christmas, that of Mary, the mother of Jesus (Luke 6:26–38). Yet, as I read the story of Zechariah's encounter with the angel Gabriel, I can't help but put myself in his place and wonder how I would react if an angel turned up to speak to me! Could we blame him for his shock, fear and doubt about the message that was brought? I think not.

As a priest, Zechariah would have known of angelic encounters from the Scriptures and even known of Gabriel from the Book of Daniel (Daniel 8:16, 9:20–21). But that day, as he woke up to prepare for his long-awaited service in the temple[65] and specifically the priestly duty of burning incense (an act to symbolise the offering of the prayers of the people), he could not have known what was in store for him.

The word 'angel' comes from the Greek *angelos*, which means messenger. In his book, Michael Heiser says the term is basically a job description and refers to a spirit being from God's heavenly host sent by God to deliver or receive a message[66]. Gabriel declared that he stood in the presence of God and was sent to speak to Zechariah (Luke 1:19). Gabriel is not the only angel named in the Bible[67]. However, the purpose here is not to go into a study of angels but to know that for His reasons, God has chosen to speak to His children throughout history by this means.

Zechariah and his wife were righteous in God's sight, having faithfully walked with Him. Yet they had not been able to conceive. For righteous Hebrews, this was a source of shame since children were seen to be a blessing from God (Psalm 127:3–5). Yet God had heard the cries of their heart and decided to send an angel to proclaim that they would indeed bear a son in their old age and that this baby would grow up to be a blessing, preparing the way for the Messiah. We know that this baby came to be known as John the Baptist, who preached in the wilderness, baptising people to repentance and eventually baptising Jesus (Luke 3:1–21).

While angels can be more than messengers[68], in the Scriptures, we see that when God sends angels to people, they proclaim significant announcements or give precise instructions[69]. They are incredibly important in the heavenly realm. However, they are never to be worshipped or prayed to. The angel that brought revelation to John on the Island of Patmos said this to him as John fell to worship him, 'You must not do that! I am a fellow servant with you and your brothers, the prophets, and with those who keep the words of this book. Worship God' (Revelation 22:9). Also, Paul warned the church of Colossae when addressing false teaching; 'Let no one disqualify you, insisting on asceticism and worship of angels, going on in detail about visions, puffed up without reason by his sensuous mind, and not holding fast to the Head, from whom the whole body, nourished and knit together through its joints and ligaments, grows with a growth that is from God' (Colossians 2:18–19).

While the Scriptures reveal human interactions and conversations with angels, angels should not be prayed to. Jesus taught His disciples to address their prayers to God, the Father, as He did. There is no biblical precedent for praying to angels or for someone saying to an angel, 'Go tell this to God for me.' Because of Jesus's blood sacrifice and resurrection, we have direct access to God. What an incredible privilege!

One other point to note is that the people who encountered angels in the Bible didn't go chasing or asking for the encounter. It just happened. We must be aware that God may want to speak to us in this way to give some special instruction, but we must not pursue angelic encounters. We must pursue God!

The writer of Hebrews encourages his readers to 'show hospitality to strangers, for thereby some have entertained angels unawares' (Hebrews 13:2). This indicates that angels can also take on the appearance of a human. Books have been written about unusual experiences of people just 'turning up' and then 'vanishing' in different situations where people are in need[70]. Pam, a dear YFC friend, related to me one such encounter her husband had. Could it have been an angel in disguise? Read the story and ponder.

The Fulton's Story — A heavenly encouragement?

It was not what I was expecting for my life when I walked down the aisle as a young bride in 1979. At the age of twenty, I had just married my high school sweetheart, Chris, and life was full of promise as we yielded ourselves to be used by God in whatever way He wished. Chris was even studying full-time at Bible college to become a pastor. Then, Chris was diagnosed with Multiple Sclerosis (MS)[71]. While this diagnosis was a blow, we didn't feel overwhelmed at the time as we trusted God to guide and provide for us. As the symptoms set in, coming in waves, receding and appearing, life became more and more challenging for Chris, and discouragement, along with the mobility issues, would become a constant battle. I, too, would have days of feeling discouraged and overwhelmed as I gave myself to support and care for my ailing husband. Yet God was faithful to uphold us and our family throughout the twenty years he battled this debilitating illness. Right until the end, we had hope that God would heal him; however, he passed away in the year 2000 after a brave fight.

While Chris was suffering from MS, he regularly needed to spend a day in the hospital for treatment. On one such day, he was feeling particularly discouraged as he sat alone in his hospital room receiving an infusion, a treatment that took several hours. At one point, he noticed what appeared to be a man walking by his door. The 'man' stopped and returned to the door of Chris's room. He gave Chris one simple message: 'Keep your faith.' He then disappeared and Chris never saw him again! Chris felt very encouraged by these words and the short visit.

When Chris returned home, he relayed the story to me, telling me he had a strong sense that the man was not a man but an angel. The encouragement he felt and the experience seemed to be other-worldly. Not only was Chris encouraged, but I also felt deeply encouraged that God would send a special messenger to my dear husband in his time of need. I asked Chris to describe the man's appearance. He shared his height, ethnicity and other features that stood out. What is incredible is that a few years later, Chris's sister (my sister-in-law) encountered a man of the same appearance in her time of need. I'll let her tell her story, which her husband verifies.

Marcia's Story

In February 2004, my husband and I travelled two hours from Fort Wayne to Indiana University (IU) Medical Center in Indianapolis. I had been diagnosed with MS by a neurologist in Fort Wayne. He had conducted a spinal tap and MRI (magnetic resonance imaging). He advised that the doctor in Indianapolis would confirm his diagnosis and give us resources to help prepare us for our future journey. Dealing with a chronic and progressive illness would require gaining knowledge.

We met with the doctor at IU, who confirmed the MS diagnosis. I felt numb. My brother had passed away after twenty years of going through the same slowly debilitating illness, so what would happen to me? Our family saw our youngest sibling go through a long, agonising loss of his ability to be autonomous, and I was fearful of the same outcome. The unknown was smothering, leaving my husband, Kevin, and I silent as we returned to our car. As we silently walked, two young men walked up behind us. It was surprising because where we walked was empty for the most part, and the two men seemed in a rush yet strode right up to us – one on each side. A cigarette aroma struck me, and I was a bit concerned about who they might be. The one who passed me said something that surprised me. He assured me God would be with me on this journey. I don't recall the exact words, but I tucked it in my mind as a way God wanted to assure me He had this. After he spoke, it seemed they both just vanished.

Kevin and I did not discuss the encounter until a few days later, in our small group Bible study. They had all prayed for me and wanted to know how the consultation had gone. We shared that the MS diagnosis was confirmed and that the doctor gave us quite a lot of information to read. As I was sharing the facts of the appointment, the memory of that encounter flooded me, and I just had to share. Once I spoke, Kevin told them how surreal the moment was. That was when I realised God had sent us His extra special touch. I've held onto that precious touch as I've dealt with my long journey with MS.

It wasn't until many years later that we heard of Chris' encounter with a man of the same appearance. In awe, I wondered if we had also met an angel in disguise on that day in 2004.

HIGHLIGHT *from* HISTORY

The Waorani tribe of Ecuador

For this 'Highlight from History', I use an example that shows God using angels indirectly to communicate. I say 'indirectly' as, in this instance, an angel or angels didn't speak directly to a person. However, their presence communicated a message that led one person, then subsequently a whole tribe, to know the good news of the gospel.

The year: 1956. The setting: the depths of the Ecuadorian jungle. A group of young male missionaries had been planning to reach an unreached tribe, whom they referred to at that time as the 'Auca Indians', for several years. This tribe was known for its brutality (Auca was the Quichua word referring to savagery), and no 'outsiders' had successfully made contact.

Two of the group, Ed McCully and Nate Saint (a pilot), had been air-dropping gifts to the Auca houses in the hopes of building friendship. They aimed to be able to approach them on the ground at a later date[72]. In the latter part of 1955, the group, including Jim Elliot, Roger Youderian and Pete Fleming, began secretly planning how to attempt a ground meeting. Jim had also been learning Auca phrases from a young woman named Dayuma (who had fled the Auca) in order to convey their friendly intentions.

Upon identifying a safe landing spot on a beach alongside the Curaray River, close to the Auca houses, Ed and Nate landed successfully on 3 January 1956[73]. After a few more trips to deliver equipment and the other men, the five of them were finally set to make land contact with the Auca. They built a shelter on the treetops and interacted with three Auca, using the phrases they knew. Journal entries and letters to their wives reveal their excitement and anticipation of meeting the rest of the tribe. However, on Sunday 8 January 1956, all radio communication went silent. Worst fears were realised when all five bodies were found later that week, killed by the spears of the very people they were trying to reach. This story of five young American missionaries being killed spread far and wide in the Western world, and was even reported in the well-known *Time* magazine.[74]

However, the story continues. Nate's sister, Rachel, was learning the Auca language and continued to do so. She and Elisabeth Elliot (Jim's wife) moved to an Auca settlement five years after the incident. Friendly relations had been resumed with the help of Dayuma[75]. While Elisabeth returned to the USA after a few years, Rachel stayed on for many decades and saw the Auca become believers and a church established[76]. While some information about the men's deaths was revealed early on in their time with the Auca, the women felt they shouldn't ask many questions about that fateful day. Dawa, a young woman, was the first of the Auca to become a Christian and, in 1989, a key factor in her decision to convert was revealed.

She had been in the jungle the day that the five men had been killed, observing the events that unfolded. After the killing, she heard unusual singing, so she looked up to the treetops to where the sound came from and saw a large group of people and what looked like a hundred flashlights[77]. The killers on the beach also heard and saw this. They were frightened by this unexpected vision. However, years later, once they understood the gospel and learned the Scriptures, they realised that what they had seen were angels[78]. Once they understood what they had seen, they were no longer afraid. God had given them a glimpse of the heavenly realm.

This vision of the angels on the beach persuaded Dawa to believe in God[79]. She was the first of many to give their lives to the Lord, including the men who killed the missionaries. What was meant for evil that day was turned for good as God 'spoke' through singing angels welcoming His children home.

Reflect

How about you? Have you ever had an unusual experience that made you suspect God may have sent an angel – even in disguise? Being spoken to by an angel is not too common today. However, I believe angels are all around, ministering to our needs. How do you view these messengers from God? What perspective may have to shift to align your view with God's?

CHAPTER FIVE

[65] In the first century, priests officiated in the temple a couple of times a year according to a rota divided into twenty-four 'courses' ('Priests and Priesthood'. *Dictionary of Jesus and the Gospels*).

[66] Heiser, Michael S. (2018). *Angels: What the Bible Really Says About God's Heavenly Host*. Lexham Press, Bellingham, p. 18.

[67] For example, Michael (Revelation 12:7–9), Lucifer (fallen angel who is Satan ... Isaiah 14:12), plus many unnamed angels.

[68] For example, protectors (Psalm 91:11), carrying out God's vengeance (Revelation 16:1), worshipers (Revelation 7:11–12).

[69] For examples see Matthew 2:13, 19; Luke 1:11–13; Luke 1:26–33; Luke 2:9–14.

[70] For example, McDonald, Hope. (1982). *When Angels Appear: Fifty Real-life Encounters with Angels*. Harper Collins, New York; Malz, Betty. (1986). *Angels by My Side*. Chosen, Minnesota.

[71] MS is an acquired neurological disease where the body's own immune system attacks the fatty material around the nerves (called myelin), which results in numerous symptoms as the nerves become exposed.

[72] Elliot, E. (1958). *Shadow of the Almighty: The life-adventure, witness, testament and glory of Jim Elliot, one of the five martyrs of Ecuador*. Hodder and Stoughton, London, p. 234.

[73] Elliot, E. (1956, 1957, 1988 Ed). *Through Gates of Splendour*. OM Publishing, UK, p. 154.

[74] *Time* magazine, 23 January 1956.

[75] Martins Miller, S. (1995). *Jim Elliot: Missionary to Ecuador*. Barbour, Ohio, p. 192.

[76] ibid.

[77] Fleming Liefeld, O. (1990). *Unfolding Destinies: The Untold Story of Peter Fleming and the Aura Mission*. Zondervan, Michigan, p. 236.

[78] ibid. p. 237.

[79] Martins Miller, S. (1995). *Jim Elliot: Missionary to Ecuador*. Barbour, Ohio, p. 195.

"Face To Face"

Chapter Six

God speaks through an audible voice

'Peter, what are you doing?' Peter went outside, thinking that his mother had called him. He went outside only to find that she hadn't. He returned to the kitchen, upset at his mother, for he was sure she had called him. The voice came again, 'Peter, what are you doing?' This time, realising it wasn't his mother's voice, he went outside to see who was calling him, but no one was there. He returned to the kitchen again, and for a third time, the voice came, 'Peter, what are you doing?' This time, the Holy Spirit spoke to Peter's heart and said, 'This is the Lord speaking to you.'

This is the story of Peter Wohangara, a then-young Indonesian teenager who heard God's voice audibly. He had become a Christian at the age of eleven but had gone his own way for a couple of years. This is how God decided to get his attention again and to give him his calling. 'I want you for my servant, and I will use you on the island of Kalimantan,' the Lord said[80].

While stories like this are not often heard, and I have never had God speak to me audibly, there is enough testament to the fact that God can and still does speak to people today in this way. Of course, there is also a biblical precedent for God speaking audibly. Let's look at the story of the great Hebrew prophet Moses.

From hiding his face to 'face to face'

> Now Moses was keeping the flock of his father-in-law, Jethro, the priest of Midian, and he led his flock to the west side of the wilderness and came to Horeb, the mountain of God. And the angel of the Lord appeared to him in a flame of fire out of the midst of a bush. He looked, and behold, the bush was burning, yet it was not consumed. And Moses said, 'I will turn aside to see this great sight, why the bush is not burned.' When the Lord saw that he turned aside to see, God called to him out of the bush, 'Moses, Moses!' And he said, 'Here I am.' Then he said, 'Do not come near; take your sandals off your feet, for the place on which you are standing is holy ground.' And he said, 'I am the God of your father, the God of Abraham, the God of Isaac, and the God of Jacob.' And Moses hid his face, for he was afraid to look at God.
> (Exodus 3:1–6)

> Now Moses used to take the tent and pitch it outside the camp, far off from the camp, and he called it the tent of

meeting. And everyone who sought the Lord would go out to the tent of meeting, which was outside the camp. Whenever Moses went out to the tent, all the people would rise up, and each would stand at his tent door, and watch Moses until he had gone into the tent. When Moses entered the tent, the pillar of cloud would descend and stand at the entrance of the tent, and the Lord would speak with Moses. And when all the people saw the pillar of cloud standing at the entrance of the tent, all the people would rise up and worship, each at his tent door. Thus the Lord used to speak to Moses face to face, as a man speaks to his friend.
(Exodus 33:7–11)

Imagine being Moses, going about your usual business of looking after the sheep, when a bush suddenly catches your attention as it's on fire! Your first instinct may be panic. Perhaps you're thinking, 'How do I put this fire out so it doesn't spread and threaten my sheep?' But you take a closer look and realise this bush is burning, but it's not burning up, nor is it spreading! If you're not already questioning your sanity and wondering if you're hallucinating, you would have even more reason to do so when you hear your name being called out from said bush.

'Moses, Moses!' You have no idea who is saying your name out in the middle of nowhere or for what purpose, but it's undeniable that you have heard it, so you better respond. Shakily, you say, 'Here I am.'

After forty years of trying to forget your past and establishing yourself in a new home with a new family, your past is about to come back and bite you. 'I am the God of your father, the God of Abraham, the God of Isaac, and the God of Jacob.' You've been trying to forget where you come from, who you are, and what you've done, but the God of your fathers hasn't forgotten you. No wonder you can't look at God. All that guilt and shame, not only for the murder you committed, but for abandoning your people, both your adoptive family and the people who are your blood, enslaved and suffering under the hands of the Egyptians. Maybe your judgement day had arrived, and you were about to be wiped out!

Even though you're too afraid to look, your ears are still open to listening. So, God continues to speak. God speaks to you about the suffering of His people in Egypt, that now is the time of their deliverance … and that you are the one He's sending to make it happen! What? No wonder you are full of questions, 'Who am I? What do I say? What if they don't believe me?' God patiently answers your questions and demonstrates His power (Exodus 3:1–6).

Fast forward, and through great signs and wonders, Pharaoh finally lets God's people, the Israelites, go. Moses led them through the parted Red Sea and is now leading them in the wilderness. No longer was Moses afraid to look at God. In fact, he now knew God intimately and met God 'face to face' as with a friend. Moses was not only God's chosen instrument for delivering His people from slavery but also for bringing God's law (His rule and order for life) to them. What began as a moment of terror when He heard God's audible voice became a life of faithful service and friendship[81]. 'And there has not arisen a prophet since in Israel like Moses, whom the Lord knew face to face ...' (Deuteronomy 34:10).

Isn't it amazing that God knew Moses's name and knows us by name? We see other stories in the Bible where God spoke people's names out of the blue. The young prophet Samuel was lying in bed when he heard God call His name. He thought it was the priest Eli, but Eli said it wasn't him each time he got up to find out (1 Samuel 3). Saul, the persecutor of Christians, was blinded and heard his name, 'Saul, Saul, why are you persecuting Me?' (Acts 9:4 NKJV). If ever you have an experience of God speaking your name audibly or saying anything at all audibly, surely it's an invitation to a great call on your life.

Hilary's Story — The great escape

Warning: This story contains graphic details of violence in wartime.

The year was 1988. I was in my third and final year of university in Sierra Leone. 'Hilary.' The voice came out of nowhere as I walked across my university campus to class. I turned around, trying to see the person who spoke my name. But there was no one there. Then I woke up. *This must be my Father.* 'You will be travelling,' came the voice again. Before I could ponder this, the voice spoke once more, 'You will become a pastor.' This was my first experience of the audible voice of

God. God spoke to me in a very real and tangible way about my calling. Both of these things have come to pass, with the travelling component starting not long after, as I was invited to travel with a YFC Africa band to the USA the following year. But the second time I experienced the audible voice of God, it was life or death.

The rebels entered the city of Freetown on 6 January 1999. Houses and churches were being burned down, and people were being hacked to death. It was horrendous what they were doing to people, even disembowelling pregnant women. We had nowhere to run to and nowhere to hide. So we had to stay put in our tiny house. One night, word came from the rebels that they would enter our neighbourhood to recruit the men. Anyone who was a man, including my wife's uncle who lived with us, took off. He said, 'Hilary, are you coming?'

I said, 'No, I'm not going anywhere. My wife and children are here; I'm not going anywhere.'

It was chaos as women started running into our compound and house while he and other men were running off. Terrified, they were yelling, 'Where's Pastor? Is Pastor here?' The women were confident they would be safe if they went to a pastor's house. So, over twenty women and some young children were crammed into our tiny house as the rebels came closer. I was the only man left. At one point, the rebels approached the house next door. I started pacing up and down, praying, even though there was hardly any room to move. One lady wanted to scream out of fear when she saw them through the window, but I told her to keep quiet. Usually, when the rebels came to a house, they would pour gasoline around the house and then set it alight. However, this time, they reached a certain point and stopped. God protected us that day.

A couple of days later, I was in the bathroom getting ready to bathe, my son was sleeping in the adjacent bedroom and my wife was outside preparing food while our daughter slept on my wife's back. We heard a heavy thud. When we looked to see what it was, we discovered that a rocket-propelled grenade had landed at the back of the house between the bedroom and the bathroom. And it didn't go off! Amazing.

One morning, not long after, I was standing on the verandah at the front of my house, which was by the side of the road that went east to west. I would see people who had gone to the east returning with no hands as the rebels were very active in the east. The Nigerian peacekeeping troops had come to the western part of the city, so people were moving west to get away from the rebels. As I was watching people coming and going, out of nowhere, I heard, 'Leave now.' Like I had ten years earlier, I turned around to see who said it. There was no one there. I thought it could have been one of the people taking refuge in our house, but no, there was nobody. I knew it was my Father. Immediately, I went inside and said to my wife, 'We're leaving now!'

'Oh, where are we going? What do you mean? What do we take with us?' she asked. I said, 'We're going to take our passports for identification. We're leaving now. We're not taking anything. The only thing you need to do is to make sure you have diapers for the kids. Take enough supplies for the kids and take what you think we need for a week or two. Let's just leave!'

Some other people, including my wife's aunt, decided to come with us. The others stayed back in our house. The journey to the west was terrifying as we had to go through Nigerian military checkpoints. If someone saw you and said that you were a rebel, they would just shoot you on the spot. Eventually, we got to a place of safety, my mum's house, and stayed there for several days. Once we were safe, I wanted to discover what had happened in our area. We found out that there had been a rampage – houses burned down, people killed. Thankfully, our house was safe. But many people in our area were killed that day. All we could do was thank God that He had directed us to leave when He did.

We were eventually able to return to the house when things settled down. The rebels terrorised the city for three weeks, but eventually, they were kicked out. Not one person who came to take refuge in our house was harmed. All glory goes to God.

HIGHLIGHT *from* HISTORY

Florence Nightingale — Nurse, statistician and social reformer

You may have heard of Florence Nightingale, known as the 'Lady with the Lamp', because of her fearless nursing of British and Allied soldiers during the Crimean War in the 1850s[82]. She became known as the founder of modern nursing, establishing the first scientific-based nursing school, which opened in London in 1860. She took meticulous notes and wrote hundreds of books and pamphlets, her most famous being *Notes on Nursing: What it is and What it is not*, which has remained in publication since 1859[83]. However, her road to working in her calling was not an easy one, with much spiritual struggle amid societal and family expectations.

Born in 1820 in Florence, Italy, while her parents were on an extended honeymoon (hence her name), Florence grew up in privileged English society. As a child, she was much more interested in her education and the suffering of the less fortunate than in the traditional female role of home management.

Her father oversaw her education and she could speak and write several languages at an early age.

In 1837, at sixteen years of age, she first felt God call her. She wrote in her notes, 'God spoke to me and called me to His service.' It was not an inward revelation … she heard an objective voice, a voice outside herself, speaking to her in human words[84]. She was not clear about what this service should be but, whenever she had the opportunity, she nursed the sick and needy. As a young lady of society, she was expected to attend all the social engagements, be courted and get married. Yet she found all the frivolities of that lifestyle dissatisfying, much to the chagrin of her mother and sister.

She earnestly sought God throughout this time, frustrated that she could not figure out this calling. With family and friends, she travelled to Rome, Egypt and Germany and, along the way, encountered people or situations that would help her to keep seeking her calling, including Catholic sisters in Rome and the Protestant-run 'Kaiserswerth' in Germany. Kaiserwerth was an institute founded in 1833 for the care of the destitute and had grown into a training school for female teachers and nurses[85]. Here, she saw models of loving care for orphans and the sick that stirred her desire to live a life of surrendered service. However, the expectations of English society and her family were a battle when she returned home[86].

It just happened that Florence's sister fell sick and was ordered to have respite in Germany. This allowed Florence to return to Germany in 1851 with her sister and mother, and she managed to return to Kaiserswerth for a four-month apprenticeship as a sick nurse[87]. Finally, in 1853, at 33 years of age, she could break free from family expectations to fully enter her calling when she was invited to manage an initiative started by a group of wealthy aristocratic ladies called the 'Institute for the Care of Sick Gentlewomen'[88]. It was sixteen years after she heard that voice before she could fully realise her calling. She later wrote that she heard this voice on three other occasions: once in 1853 before going to her first post at the Hospital for the Poor Gentlewomen, once in 1854 before going to Crimea to nurse the soldiers and once in 1861 after a good friend died[89].

Florence's determination to follow the call of God, no matter the pull of societal expectations, has left a lasting legacy in health care worldwide. She was called and sustained by God throughout her life, saying, 'If I could give you information of my life, it would be to show how a woman of very ordinary ability has been led by God in strange and unaccustomed paths to do in His service what He has done in her. And if I could tell you all, you would see how God has done all, and I nothing. I have worked hard, very hard, that is all; and I have never refused God anything[90].'

Reflect

How about you? Have you ever heard God's audible voice? Or do you know someone who has? I know only a couple of people who have had this experience. Yet, whether He speaks audibly or in 'a still, small voice' (1 Kings 19:11–13), will you be willing to heed the call no matter the cost? Take courage; He who calls will also sustain.

[80] Mel Tari as told to Chris Dudley. (1971). *Like a Mighty Wind*. Creation House, Illinois, pp. 142–143.

[81] Read Moses's story in Exodus, Leviticus, Numbers and Deuteronomy.

[82] https://www.britannica.com/biography/Florence-Nightingale (Accessed 9 May 2024).

[83] ibid.

[84] Woodham-Smith, C. (1968 edition). *Florence Nightingale*, 1820–1910. Fontana Books, London, p. 21.

[85] https://victorianweb.org/victorian/history/crimea/florrie.html (Accessed 9 May 2024).

[86] Wellman, S. (1999). *Florence Nightingale: Lady with the Lamp*. Barbour, Ohio, pp. 121–135.

[87] https://victorianweb.org/victorian/history/crimea/florrie.html (Accessed 9 May 2024).

[88] Wellman, S. (1999). *Florence Nightingale: Lady with the Lamp*. Barbour, Ohio, pp. 136–137.

[89] Woodham-Smith, C. (1968 edition). *Florence Nightingale*, 1820–1910. Fontana Books, London, p. 22.

[90] https://www.goodreads.com/quotes/265726-if-i-could-give-you-information-of-my-life-it (Accessed 4 March, 2025.)

"He Reveals Deep And Secret Things"

Chapter Seven

God speaks through people

It was 2008. I was on a missions trip, leading a school holiday programme in a small Aboriginal community within Darwin[91]. At the same time, some other interstate guests were visiting and helping the local church. After one of the services, one of these guests, an older lady, asked if she could pray for me. As she prayed, she said, 'I see you like a Cindy Jacobs and that these hands are hands of healing. One day, you will pray for people, and they will be healed.' At that stage, I had no idea who Cindy Jacobs was, so I had to do some research. I saw that she was an international intercessor who had written books on prayer. I also had never seen anyone healed when I had prayed for them. I guess I just put this word 'on the shelf' and didn't think about it much, as my focus for the next few years was working alongside Aboriginal people, especially youth. As the years progressed, I did start to see people healed as I prayed for them. The first was a man who had travelled to the Northern Territory to serve at a youth camp and had a swollen and painful knee. Eventually, through the Lord's leading and twelve years after this word was given, I became the International Prayer Director for Youth for Christ and started writing about prayer. I can't even remember this lady's name (until now, I have never come across her again), but I often think about the word she gave me that day and how God has been faithful to lead me into His plans and purpose for my life. It has greatly encouraged me when I feel inadequate for the task or when things get hard. God has always used people to speak, from the prophets of old to your local pastor, from authors and artists to poets and musicians. God can use anyone who is willing to hear and obey.

Nothing is hidden from God

And the Lord sent Nathan to David. He came to him and said to him, 'There were two men in a certain city, the one rich and the other poor. The rich man had very many flocks and herds, but the poor man had nothing but one little ewe lamb, which he had bought. And he brought it up, and it grew up with him and with his children. It used to eat of his morsel and drink from his cup and lie in his arms, and it was like a daughter to him. Now there came a traveller to the rich man, and he was unwilling to take one of his own flock or herd to prepare for the guest who had come to him, but he took the poor man's lamb and prepared it for the man who had come to him.' Then David's anger was greatly kindled against the man, and he said to Nathan, 'As the Lord lives, the man who has done this deserves to die, and he shall

restore the lamb fourfold, because he did this thing, and because he had no pity.'
Nathan said to David, 'You are the man!…David said to Nathan, 'I have sinned against the Lord.' And Nathan said to David, 'The Lord also has put away your sin; you shall not die. Nevertheless, because by this deed you have utterly scorned the Lord, the child who is born to you shall die.' Then Nathan went to his house.
(2 Samuel 12:1–7a, 13-15).

I hesitated to use this example from the Bible to show how God can use other people to speak. You see, it isn't the most comfortable of messages to consider. We like uplifting and encouraging messages; don't get me wrong, the majority of the time that we hear from God through others will indeed be encouraging and uplifting, just like when God used the lady in Darwin to speak to me. But sometimes we need convicting and disciplining, just as Hebrews says, 'the LORD disciplines those He loves' (Hebrews 12:6 NLT).

Nathan and David already had an established relationship as prophet and king so it was Nathan's right to speak into David's life in this way (See 2 Samuel 7, 1 Chronicles 17). He doesn't say outright what God has revealed to him but uses a parable of outrageous injustice to play on David's emotions, setting David up for the truth of his unjust actions. The tactic worked, and David came to repentance, which is the desired outcome for any correctional message. We know that David was a man after God's own heart (Acts 13:22) therefore, his repentance was genuine and deep, as evidenced by the poem he wrote in the aftermath of this incident:

> Have mercy on me, O God,
> > because of your unfailing love.
> Because of your great compassion,
> > blot out the stain of my sins.
> Wash me clean from my guilt.
> > Purify me from my sin.
> For I recognize my rebellion;
> > it haunts me day and night.
> Against you, and you alone, have I sinned;
> > I have done what is evil in your sight.
> You will be proved right in what you say,
> > and your judgment against me is just.
>
> (Psalm 51:1–4 NLT – read the whole chapter for more context)

Nathan was faithful in delivering the message of the Lord, no matter how difficult it may have been or what reaction he may have received from David. The Lord may want to use you to deliver a challenging message to someone. If that is the case, much prayer and certainty in your spirit must be there before giving such a message; if the person is immature or not wholeheartedly committed to God, then there is potential for spiritual damage. In the end, obedience to God is the most important thing, and the person's reaction needs to be left to God.

God can also use other people to help guide, warn and prepare people for what's to come (See Acts 11:27–30 as an example). Of course, God can use people to speak to others through the gifts they have been given, whether through a book they have written, a painting, a song or even a movie or play. Just think of all the letters Paul wrote to bring God's instruction to others and David's psalms (songs) written to express his innermost praise and pain. God is so gracious in using imperfect human beings to deliver His messages.

Let's hear how one YFC worker from Canada has tuned herself into the voice of God through the purposeful contemplation of other people's art.

Vivienne's Story — Hearing God through art

I've always struggled with a real love/hate relationship with words. I want to use words to express the inner movements in my soul, but then I get frustrated because there don't seem to be enough words or the right ones to touch on the inner spaces within my life. In prayer, I find words so often feel insufficient to articulate my emotions and sentiments. In the past, I've found much comfort and connection with God through creative prayer expressions such as dance movement, impromptu singing and artistic creating.

When words fail me, I thank God for giving me senses that communicate with Him beyond my speaking – looking out upon a landscape or stooping to sniff a flower. I often find myself stopping to smile up at the sky in a moment of secret thankfulness.

The more I can carry prayer with me in the simple moments of my day through creative cooking, home tidying or watering plants – the more I find my mind turning back to God's constant companionship.

With this revelation has come the realisation that I am a creator – one who enjoys creating beauty, order and goodness in the world around me. Though my creative powers are pretty limited compared to the Creator – for He speaks matter into being, and I simply rearrange it – I find that I connect with God deeply as I embrace my gift as a creative being and look to Him for the shape of living well in that identity.

Many people feel that if they can't hold a paintbrush to make a piece of art, they aren't creative. But I am joyfully finding more and more that I can be an artist in all things: the way I combine ingredients to make a meal, the way I set out space to welcome guests, the way I group ideas in my mind and heart. I truly believe I was designed to be an artist in all my ways.

It shouldn't have come as such a surprise then when I noticed that art was where God reached out to me in prayer conversations. When words failed to give shape to my deepest yearnings, I found that God related to me through pieces of art. Calming my noisy mind, drawing my senses towards a focused idea, and inviting me to sit still in His presence; the gift of sitting with art as a form of faithful waiting before the Lord became part of my prayer rhythm.

For a few years now, I've been meeting with a group of friends for fifteen minutes on a Zoom call to sit together with the Lord and a piece of art. We rotate the piece of art each month and include a Scripture verse and a simple prayer from someone in our faith history.

The art selections range from ancient to modern but always depict God in action – whether descending as flames of fire during Pentecost or walking with His disciples on the road to Emmaus. There are so many ways to let art illustrate God's history with us as Scripture tells the story.

One particular piece was a modern Ukrainian icon of Jesus as the Word of God, speaking creation into being. In a circular shape, Jesus's face filled the top third of the circle, looking down upon the work of His Word. Beneath, seven days of creation stood side by side, cradled in His giant hands: moon and stars, vegetation, animals, ocean and humans. Week after week, I sat with this piece of art, feeling myself invited into the illustration. I felt myself laying on my back in the palm of God's hand, being smiled upon by the face of Christ at creation.

'I love you. I created you out of my love. You are a unique expression of my intentional love.'

The words rang deep into parts of me that needed to be reassured, healed, and held.

Through the wordless art of another human, God was able to get my attention and remind me that He is holding me, creating me in an ongoing work of love. My defences melted; I was a small bundle of love in the arms of the Creator, soaking in Christ's gaze.

Not every piece of art awakens my heart to God's voice. But as I faithfully hold this rhythm of prayer with my friends, I feel a very real stilling of my heart and receptivity to the Holy Spirit brooding over me.

Often, God uses the weekly 'Visio Divina' – as we've come to call it – to remind me of the simplest truths: that I am known, that His love shapes me and that I often resist His love.

Rather than finding big wordy prayers to respond to God, I notice that my heart's inner posture is shifting, like a sunflower turning towards the sun. My heart is a space of hospitality for the Holy Spirit, and I notice the signs of His creative work in my soul more and more. Forgiveness flows more naturally, peaceful responses to chaos seem more normal and generosity beyond my natural norm is more frequent.

I'm learning to be a creator by following the hints and clues of the Creator. Yes!

HIGHLIGHT *from* HISTORY

William Wilberforce — Politician and social reformer

William Wilberforce is one of my favourite historical figures. Halfway through a biography about his life, I was inspired to pray, 'Lord, what would you have me give myself to for the rest of my life?' His response has set the course of my life since.

William Wilberforce was a man of great persistence who fought for the abolition of the slave trade and, eventually, the abolition of slavery itself amid great personal health struggles and political opposition. It took twenty years from his first becoming a politician and taking up this cause to see his bill for the abolition of the slave trade passed in March 1807. This may not have happened if God hadn't used his spiritual mentor, John Newton, to speak to him.

William Wilberforce was born in 1759 in Hull, Yorkshire, to a wealthy merchant family. When he was eight, his father passed away, and he was sent to London to live with an aunt and uncle. It was here, at the age of eleven, that he first met John Newton, the former slave trader turned Anglican clergyman. They immediately took a liking to each other. However, his family back in Hull didn't like that he was being influenced by the Methodism of his aunt and uncle and, therefore, brought him back to Hull and sent him to another school. His initial enthusiasm for God waned, and he found himself caught up in society's social life, such as in theatre, card playing and balls. During his time at Cambridge University, he was known to have a hedonistic lifestyle and paid little attention to his studies. It wasn't until more than ten years after their initial meeting that Newton came back into Wilberforce's life.

Wilberforce entered politics as a twenty-four-year-old and began to go on a spiritual journey, largely thanks to a tour of Europe in 1784–85 with Isaac Milner (the younger brother of his previous school principal in Hull). During this time, they read *The Rise and Progress of Religion in the Soul* by Philip Doddridge, and Wilberforce began to read the Bible. He was converted to Christ and went through such a spiritual struggle that he contemplated quitting politics to enter the clergy. At that time, he sought counsel from Newton, who urged him to stay in politics and encouraged him that God could use him in Parliament.

Many years later, in 1796, Wilberforce was on the verge of quitting politics after yet another defeat of his abolition of the slave trade bill. Not only was he feeling defeated in politics, but he was going through another severe bout of illness and depression when he reached out to his spiritual mentor. Again, Newton's wise words, full of biblical encouragement, were what Wilberforce needed to hear to persevere in his call to politics[92]. A further eleven years later, the bill was finally passed, and

CHAPTER SEVEN   117

Wilberforce took his place in history. He continued to campaign for the abolition of slavery. In the English summer of 1833, Parliament passed the second reading of the Emancipation Act, ensuring the end of slavery in the British Empire. Three days later, Wilberforce died[93].

As well as being used to help end slavery, he was consistently involved in church work that included the Church Missionary Society and the sending of missionaries to India and Africa; the British and Foreign Bible Society; the Proclamation Society Against Vice and Immorality; the School Society; the Sunday School Society; the Bettering Society; the Vice Society and others. His public philanthropic efforts were vast and included relieving the suffering of the manufacturing poor, French refugees and foreigners in distress. He made significant financial contributions to at least seventy such societies, many bearing his name as an officer. History records Wilberforce as having been active in numerous reform movements, which included reform in hospital care, fever institutions, asylums, infirmaries, refugees and penitentiaries[94]. And one of my personal favourites is the first-ever animal welfare society in the world, the Society for the Prevention of Cruelty to Animals[95].

God used one man's words to encourage another man to continue his calling, impacting the entire British Empire and countless people ... and animals!

Reflect

How about you? Who could you come alongside to be 'God's voice' to today? Perhaps there's a song you need to compose, a painting you need to paint or a dance you need to dance that God will use to speak to someone at the exact moment they need to help them persevere in faith and calling. May you be open to hearing from God for others and to receiving what God has to say through others.

CHAPTER SEVEN   119

[91] Darwin is the small capital city of the Northern Territory, Australia.

[92] To read the letter go to: https://www.christianitytoday.com/history/issues/issue-93/you-have-not-labored-in-vain.html (Accessed 23 April 2024).

[93] Pierard, R. (1997). 'William Wilberforce: Fighting the Slave Trade', *Christianity Today*, Issue 53. https://www.christianitytoday.com/history/issues/issue-53/william-wilberforce-and-abolition-of-slave-trade-did-you.html (Accessed 23 April 2024).

[94] Gathro, R. (2001). 'William Wilberforce and His Circle of Friends', Summer issue of the C. S. *Lewis Institute Report*. https://www.cslewisinstitute.org/wp-content/uploads/KD-2001-Summer-William-Wilberforce-and-His-Circle-of-Friends-471.pdf (Accessed 23 April 2024).

[95] Wikipedia. 'RSPCA': https://en.wikipedia.org/wiki/RSPCA#:~:text=The%20society%20was%20the%20first,Animals%2C%20as%20it%20is%20today (Accessed 23 April 2024).

"Let Us Cast Lots"

Chapter Eight

God speaks through circumstances

In my early twenties, I thought God might have been calling me to be a missionary teacher. The thought was triggered by a visit to good friends who had gone to be medical missionaries in Nepal. Later the same year, I went to Bible School in Canada and, as part of the school, I had an opportunity to take a mission trip to Mexico. While I loved my time there, I was so frustrated at not being able to speak the language, and unfortunately, I didn't seem to have any gift to pick up language easily. I remember saying to God, 'I don't know if I could do this,' but I was fully surrendered to whatever He may have had in store. The first week back at Bible School after the trip, one of the classes was on the book of Ezekiel. As the teacher read aloud a passage one day, a verse stood out to me like a sore thumb:

'For you are not being sent to a people of unintelligible speech or difficult language, but to the house of Israel, nor to many peoples of unintelligible speech or difficult language, whose words you cannot understand. But I have sent you to the people who understand you;' (Ezekiel 3:5–6 NASB).

I just had to laugh to myself and say, 'Thank you, God.' God used a combination of my circumstances and His written Word to give me clear direction on what not to do. God can and will use a series of events, situations or experiences to speak to us.

Not the kind of circumstance you want!

The word of the Lord came to Jonah the son of Amittai, saying, "Arise, go to Nineveh, the great city, and cry out against it, because their wickedness has come up before Me." But Jonah got up to flee to Tarshish from the presence of the Lord. So he went down to Joppa, found a ship that was going to Tarshish, paid the fare, and boarded it to go with them to Tarshish away from the presence of the Lord.
However, the Lord hurled a great wind on the sea and there was a great storm on the sea, so that the ship was about to break up. ... And each man said to his mate, "Come, let's cast lots so that we may find out on whose account this catastrophe has struck us." So they cast lots, and the lot fell on Jonah. ... And he said to them, "Pick me up and hurl me into the sea. Then the sea will become calm for you, because I know that on account of me this great storm has come upon you." ... So they picked up Jonah and hurled him into the sea, and the sea stopped its raging. Then the

men became extremely afraid of the Lord, and they offered a sacrifice to the Lord and made vows.

And the Lord designated a great fish to swallow Jonah, and Jonah was in the stomach of the fish for three days and three nights.

(Jonah 1:1-4, 7, 12, 15-17 NIV)

Jonah is the story of the prophet of God who ran away from his calling only to be swallowed by a big fish sent by God to get him to deliver the message He wanted him to. We see circumstance written all over this familiar story, yet I do not want to focus on Jonah here. Instead, I want to focus on the sailors who unknowingly picked up a rebel prophet and found themselves in terrifying circumstances.

Jonah knew God's voice, knew that He was deliberately disobeying God's voice and knew the answer to why the storm was raging (who in the heck could sleep in a boat in a storm anyway, besides Jesus! – see Mark 4:38). On the other hand, the sailors didn't know the one true God, but this storm certainly got their attention. Crying out to their gods didn't work, so they wanted this stranger to call on his God. When they cast lots (an ancient way of determining decisions, in this case, the identity of a guilty party[96]), it fell to Jonah, another circumstance. They knew Jonah would have the answer as to what to do to save their lives. Interestingly, Jonah didn't cry out to God to stop the storm. The sailors didn't like his answer, trying to take things into their own hands by rowing to the shore to get rid of him.

Yet the storm grew greater, the circumstances grew worse, and finally, they did what Jonah said to do by throwing him overboard. Immediately, the storm stopped. Now, God really had their attention. They 'became extremely afraid of the Lord, and they offered a sacrifice to the Lord and made vows' (Jonah 1:16). Their fear of death before became an introduction to the fear of the Lord when they saw that the God of the Israelites was indeed the God who made the earth and sea and had control over the elements. Right then, they sacrificed to the one true God and made vows, a solemn promise, perhaps even consecrating themselves to now serve Him rather than the gods they had previously worshipped.

This is a dramatic example of how God used circumstances to speak to a group of men who didn't know Him. They were not seeking God out; they were going about their usual lives when an unexpected event introduced them to Him. At other times, God may use circumstances in response to prayer, such as when Gideon threw the fleece of wool on the threshing floor and asked God firstly to put dew on the fleece only and not on the ground and then the next night, to put dew on the ground only and not on the fleece (Judges 6:36–40).

If the circumstances aren't as dramatic, it may be easy to miss God's voice as we often think that 'life just happens', and we don't take time to reflect on what God might be teaching us. Jack Deere says, in *Surprised by the Voice of God*, 'Although the voice of God runs through all experiences, most of us have diligently trained ourselves to ignore His voice and get on with the business of life'[97]. Jaimi Winship suggests asking God, when going through challenging circumstances, 'What do you want me to know about this situation?' and 'What do you want me to do about it?[98]' Taking time to reflect and ask these questions will help us tune into His voice through circumstance.

Matheus' and Muriel's Story — Divine alignment

NOTE – MPC are the initials for YFC in Portuguese.

Muriel and I met as teenagers. We came to know the Lord after we married in our early twenties. We have been married for eighteen years and have two beautiful children. I have been a physical educator, teacher and coach for twenty years. Muriel is also a teacher and an educational counsellor. We had a very comfortable life in Brazil, serving in leadership in our church and working hard in our jobs. Circumstances in our lives started to shift in 2017 when we were first introduced to MPC. Muriel had taken up a position in a new school in 2015. While at this school, she sought ways to help the teenagers with their challenges, which led her to meet the staff of MPC in our town to discuss what could be done. A passion for the work of MPC developed immediately. Soon after, we were involved in the core team, planning and organising activities in various schools in the city. The kingdom focus, working with people from different churches to love and introduce young people to Jesus, awakened us and changed our lives as people, parents and teachers. Then, God began to speak very clearly to us about our calling as missionaries.

One afternoon in 2021, I attended a lecture by the School of Life project (a ministry of MPC Brazil), and I realised that God was calling me to many schools, not just one. So, I reduced my teaching hours to be more available to work with MPC. Muriel remained at her job, but we moved our children from where I was teaching to her school and carried on as usual. However, during our holidays, we began going on mission trips to work with the riverine peoples of the Amazon.

Then, in January 2022, I participated in the MPC Brazil leadership training in Minas Gerais. Muriel stayed in Rio Grande do Sul with our children. During one of the mission-focused services, I was praying alone, and the colours red and green came to my mind. The Holy Spirit whispered, 'Apply for your passports.' Even though I didn't understand, I remained in prayer and asked God to confirm with Muriel if what I felt He was saying was really from Him. So, on the Saturday night, I called her and asked her to pray that God would speak to her. I said nothing else because I didn't want to influence her prayer. On Sunday, after praying, she felt the Lord direct her to search the internet for preaching, and a church in Portugal appeared as her first choice. This was the first indication from God to her that He was guiding us towards Portugal.

The very next day, she was invited by a friend to go to a prayer meeting at the house of a pastor she didn't know. When she arrived at the gate, the pastor said to her, 'Welcome, missionary.' Again, she listened and was attentive to what the

Lord might want to say. During the meeting, this pastor, who didn't know Muriel or me, received a word from God and prayed for my wife, saying, 'God tells me to tell you that He wants you and your family in the nations, so get your passports ready, because He's in a hurry.'

When my wife opened her eyes, she noticed this pastor had draped a cloak over her head. On the centre of the cloak was an image of a lion, and flags from different countries were around it. The first flag that jumped out at her was the flag of Portugal. As soon as she got home, she rang me and told me everything.

I immediately spoke to my MPC leader, who was also at the training, and he pointed out that there were some participants from Portugal. I went to talk to one of them. She told me they were praying because the couple working at MPC Portugal wanted to return to Brazil and they needed someone to work on the holiday project developed by MPC Portugal. They hadn't found anyone to replace them because the person was required to be a physical educator. When she asked me what I did for a living, and I said I was a physical education teacher, she cried. Inevitably, I began to cry, too.

It was real! The Father was calling our entire family to be missionaries in Portugal. Throughout 2022, we spent a lot of time praying and fasting. My wife tried to take leave from her work numerous times, but they refused her requests. I decided to go to Portugal alone in August 2022; I spent 70 days there working with MPC ministries. When I returned to Brazil, I resigned from my job. Through prayer and fasting, we realised

God was telling us to leave everything – our jobs, home, family, and friends. So my wife resigned too.

During this time, we had many obstacles; after all, most people don't understand what drives a couple with a well-structured family to leave their guaranteed salaries and comfortable lives to go to a different country to live on offerings and serve the Lord full-time. We went through many difficult situations, but in February 2023, we arrived in Portugal.

Renunciation is an integral part of obedience, but the certainty of being at the centre of the Lord's will and the certainty that HE IS IN CONTROL of everything overcomes our fears, longings and absences. I'll close by quoting Mark 16:15: 'And he said to them, "Go into all the world and preach the gospel to everyone."' We understand that God has called us to be a response; He has found in us a willing heart, and even though He doesn't need us to do His work, He loves us so much that he invites us to be part of it.

HIGHLIGHT *from* HISTORY

John Wesley — Revivalist

John Wesley, the founder of the Methodist movement in England in the eighteenth century (and later the Methodist church), was well known for his open-air preaching to the masses. He often began preaching at 5 am and preached thrice daily. In an age without trains or automobiles, he rode over 250,000[99] miles on horseback (a distance of ten circuits of the globe) to preach salvation through Christ.

He was born into a strict Anglican family in 1703 and, at the age of seven, was pulled from a burning building by a neighbour, an act he later saw as being for a purpose – to serve God[100]. He was well educated (he mastered at least seven languages)[101], attended Oxford College with his brother Charles and became a curate in the Anglican Church. After working alongside his father in the Church for a couple of years, he returned to Oxford for further studies and resumed leadership of 'the Holy Club', a group started by Charles. Their fellow students gave this club the name in mockery of their emphasis on devotions, and it was the first sign of what would become Methodism[102].

'The Holy Club members fasted until 3 pm on Wednesdays and Fridays, received Holy Communion once each week, studied and discussed the Greek New Testament and the Classics each evening in a member's room, visited (after 1730) prisoners and the sick, and systematically brought all their lives under strict review'[103].

Despite all this, Wesley did not have a saving faith, and a series of circumstances eventually led him to his conversion in May of 1738. Most events that led him to this point were interactions with Moravian Christians[104] from Germany. One such outstanding situation was when he was en route to the Colony of Georgia (USA) in 1736. A furious storm hit the ship on which they sailed. With the main-sail smashed and water pouring over the deck, the English passengers were screaming in fear for their lives. However, the Moravians continued calmly singing a psalm that had started their usual service. The difference in demeanour struck Wesley so much. In his journal, he wrote:

> I asked one of them afterwards, 'Was you not afraid?' He answered, 'I thank God, no.' I asked, 'But were not your women and children afraid?' He replied, mildly, 'No; our women and children are not afraid to die.'
> From them I went to their crying, trembling neighbours, and pointed out to them the difference in the hour of trial, between him that feareth God, and him that feareth him not. At twelve the wind fell. This was the most glorious day which I have hitherto seen[105].

He was put in circumstance after circumstance where he had the opportunity to observe the behaviour of the Moravian Christians, their service to others, and their humility:

> 'They had put away all anger and strife, and wrath, and bitterness, and clamour, and evil-speaking; they walked worthy of the vocation wherewith they were called, and adorned the Gospel of our Lord in all things'[106].

In 1738, upon returning to England from Georgia, Wesley had a circumstance where he felt in imminent danger of death:

> 'I was strongly convinced that the cause of that uneasiness was unbelief; and that the gaining a true, living faith was the "one thing needful" for me'[107].

Again, God used a Moravian. Peter Boehler encouraged Wesley to put his faith in Christ alone for the peace he sought. On 24 May 1738, Wesley read a couple of Scriptures that spoke to him and, in the evening, he reluctantly went to a society meeting where a person read from Luther's preface to the book of Romans. All of these circumstances led to the point where, at this time, Wesley was able to pronounce,

> About a quarter before nine, while he was describing the change which God works in the heart through faith in Christ, I felt my heart strangely warmed. I felt I did trust in Christ, Christ alone for salvation: And an assurance was given me, that he had taken away my sins, even mine, and saved me from the law of sin and death[108].

Wesley's salvation led to the salvation of thousands around the globe through his faithful preaching of the good news of the gospel.

Reflect

How about you? Have you had circumstances that made you sit up and take notice? Maybe it was a severe trial you went through, you keep running into the same people all the time, or you keep trying to go for a specific job and a door shuts firmly in your face every time. Whatever circumstances have happened or will happen, take time to reflect and keep your ears open to the sound of God in this way.

CHAPTER EIGHT 133

[96] 'Lots'. Eerdman's Dictionary of the Bible.

[97] Deere, J. (1996). *Surprised by the Voice of God*. Zondervan, Grand Rapids, p. 117.

[98] Winship, J. (2019). *Hearing God's Voice* (Part 2 of 4), 'Discovering Your God-Given Identity' (24:00 following). https://www.youtube.com/watch?v=dtcrib47r0A&t=29s (Accessed 24 April 2024).

[99] 402,336 kilometres.

[100] *Christianity Today/Christian History Magazine*, (1983). 'Revival and Revolution': https://www.christianitytoday.com/history/issues/issue-2/revival-and-revolution.html (Accessed 24 April 2024).

[101] ibid.

[102] *Christianity Today/Christian History Magazine*, (1983). 'The Holy Club': https://www.christianitytoday.com/history/issues/issue-2/holy-club.html (Accessed 24 April 2024).

[103] ibid.

[104] The Moravians were a community of Christians from Hernhutt, present North East Germany. It was started by Count Zinzendorf when some religious refugees came from Moravia (present day Czechia) looking for land to settle on.

[105] Christian History Institute (1982). 'The Moravians and John Wesley': https://christianhistoryinstitute.org/magazine/article/moravians-and-wesley (Accessed 24 April 2024).

[106] ibid.

[107] ibid.

[108] ibid.

"Cross Over"

Chapter Nine

God speaks through the Spirit of Jesus/Holy Spirit

But he who enters by the door is the shepherd of the sheep. To him the gatekeeper opens. The sheep hear his voice, and he calls his own sheep by name and leads them out. When he has brought out all his own, he goes before them, and the sheep follow him, for they know his voice.
(John 10:2–4)

The works that I do in my Father's name bear witness about me, but you do not believe because you are not among my sheep. *My sheep hear my voice, and I know them, and they follow me* [my emphasis]. I give them eternal life, and they will never perish, and no one will snatch them out of my hand. My Father, who has given them to me, is greater than all, and no one is able to snatch them out of the Father's hand. I and the Father are one.
(John 10:25–30)

> Long ago, at many times and in many ways, God spoke to our fathers by the prophets, but in these last days he has spoken to us by his Son, whom he appointed the heir of all things, through whom also he created the world. He is the radiance of the glory of God and the exact imprint of his nature, and he upholds the universe by the word of his power.
> (Hebrews 1:1–3)

> When the Spirit of truth comes, he will guide you into all the truth, for he will not speak on his own authority, but whatever he hears he will speak, and he will declare to you the things that are to come. He will glorify me, for he will take what is mine and declare it to you. All that the Father has is mine; therefore I said that he will take what is mine and declare it to you.
> (John 16:13–15)

'Are you having nightmares?' I asked a teenager I had just met while visiting a local youth detention centre, where I regularly ministered.

'How did you know?' he responded with somewhat defensive interest.

I was hanging out and chatting with a group of teenagers in the detention centre, and at the same time, I was talking with God to see if there was anything He wanted to bring up or encourage them with. I felt compelled to speak with this young man, in particular. On the outside, he seemed rough and challenging, but that initial prayer – asking God what I should start the conversation with – broke down the walls and led to an in-depth discussion about God and how to have a relationship with Him. I was also able to pray the nightmares would leave and that this young man would be able to sleep in peace[109].

The simple answer to his question of how I knew about the nightmares he was having? I knew because the Holy Spirit had spoken one word into my mind: 'nightmares'. When we partner with God in ministry by listening to and following His voice, breakthroughs occur.

The Holy Spirit on mission

> Now there were in the church at Antioch prophets and teachers, Barnabas, Simeon who was called Niger, Lucius of Cyrene, Manaen a lifelong friend of Herod the tetrarch and Saul. While they were worshiping the Lord and fasting, the *Holy Spirit said* [my emphasis], 'Set apart for me Barnabas and Saul for the work to which I have called them.' Then after fasting and praying they laid their hands on them and sent them off.
> (Acts 13:1–3)

> And they went through the region of Phrygia and Galatia, *having been forbidden by the Holy Spirit* [my emphasis] to speak the word in Asia. And when they had come up to Mysia, they attempted to go into Bithynia, but the *Spirit of Jesus* [my emphasis] did not allow them. So, passing by Mysia, they went down to Troas. And a vision appeared to Paul in the

night: a man of Macedonia was standing there, urging him and saying, 'Come over to Macedonia and help us.' And when Paul had seen the vision, immediately we sought to go on into Macedonia, concluding that God had called us to preach the gospel to them.
(Acts 16:6–10)

Besides the Scriptures, I propose that the most common way that God speaks to us is directly to our spirit through the indwelling Holy Spirit. Unlike the prophets of the old covenant, who had the Holy Spirit poured out upon them for a moment in time to speak God's word and then departed, those who have been 'born again' (John 3:1–5) by the Spirit of God post the resurrection of Christ have come into union with God Himself (Romans 8:9–11, 1 Corinthians 6:17, 19, John 17:20–26, Colossians 1:27, John 14:20). Paul states this simply in his first letter to the Corinthian church when explaining the dangers of sexual immorality. Just as a man and woman become 'one flesh' in the act of sexual intercourse, in the spiritual sense, we become one with Christ, 'But he who is joined to the Lord becomes one spirit with Him' (1 Corinthians 6:17). The Spirit of the living Christ has made His home in us, this perishing earthly body (1 Corinthians 6:19). What a thought!

With that in mind, it makes sense that the Spirit of God within us would use our human faculties, such as our thoughts, imagination, physical senses and emotions, to speak to us. You may have heard different names for this, such as 'impressions', the 'inner voice' of God, or even a 'gut feeling', similar to intuition.

Jack Deere puts it this way, 'Supernatural revelatory impressions are similar to intuition in that they both communicate direct knowledge without any rational evidence or logical inference to support that knowledge. Impressions from the Holy Spirit are *different* than intuition in respect to their origin. A divine impression comes to us from the Holy Spirit, while intuition arises from within our human spirit'[110]. Jesus demonstrated an example of this when Mark tells us that Jesus 'perceived in His spirit' what a group of scribes were thinking when they saw Jesus forgive the sins of a paralytic man (Mark 2:6–8).

You may have heard of people referring to a 'picture in their mind' as a means by which God speaks. This is the use of the imagination. Of course, the imagination can be used in all sorts of unholy ways. However, believers who are 'in the Spirit' (Romans 8:9) have an imagination that has been sanctified, which means 'made holy, purified, consecrated'[111]. Paul says to the church members in Corinth, 'But you were washed, you were sanctified, you were justified in the name of the Lord Jesus Christ and by the Spirit of our God' (1 Corinthians 6:11). In relation to discerning and understanding spiritual truth, Paul even states that 'we have the mind of Christ' (1 Corinthians 2:16). How extraordinary! Richard Foster says, 'God created us with an imagination, and as Lord of his creation, he can and does redeem it and use it for the work of the kingdom of God'[112].

I believe our imagination can be trained through spiritual discipline and practice to hear the Holy Spirit this way. Early on in my walk of hearing the voice of God through the Holy Spirit, I could not picture things in my mind. However, I would receive 'words of knowledge', as demonstrated by the story at the beginning of this chapter – clear words coming into my mind that didn't originate with my own thoughts. As time progressed, I received 'word pictures' – sentences that described something – and now I can imagine scenes in my mind. While the aim of this book isn't to present tools for learning how to hear God's voice, I will mention one beneficial tool here to start practising this way of listening to God. It is called 'Ignatian Gospel Contemplation'[113], which St. Ignatius developed in the sixteenth century. It is a way of engaging the imagination while reading stories in the gospels where Jesus mixed with other people. It involves picturing yourself in the scene and using all your senses to imagine what it would have been like to be there. It leads to an imaginative engagement with Jesus in which you see what He's doing or hear what He's saying concerning you. It is a powerful tool, and I have cried many times when I have done this because of what Jesus said to me.

As mentioned, the Lord can use *all* of your senses to speak. One extraordinary experience I had in my late twenties was when God used my sense of smell to get my attention. One night, I was lying in bed when I suddenly smelt this horrible smell – like dirty socks! I looked to either side of my bed to see if I had left any dirty socks or clothes lying around. There was nothing there. Immediately, the Holy Spirit said, 'That is the smell of filthy rags' (see Isaiah 64:6). But that wasn't the end of it. I had another foul odour come across me, but this time it was like rotten eggs (if you have ever been to Rotorua in New Zealand, you'll know the smell). It's the smell of sulphur gas, and I immediately thought of how the Bible describes God pouring His judgement out through sulphur (see Revelation 14:9–11 as an example). Combining these two thoughts, the Lord made it clear that there is a judgement for sin. A sobering revelation indeed.

As we reflect on the Scriptures above, we are not told in the text *how* the Holy Spirit spoke to the prophets and teachers of the church at Antioch or *how* He prevented Paul, Timothy and Silas from going into Asia and Bithynia. However, we could speculate that it was by giving them thoughts in their mind, or in the case of forbidding them to go to specific regions, perhaps it was an unsettled feeling. It could be a combination of things; however, if it was by some other kind of supernatural means, Luke (the author of Acts) could have stated it plainly since he was unafraid to do so in retelling other accounts. Even later in the same passage in Acts 16, Luke states that Paul was given a 'vision in the night' (Acts 16:9–10).

When it comes to the more supernatural ways of God speaking to us, the Holy Spirit brings meaning to what we may have 'seen or heard'. For example, if God gives a dream, that dream often needs interpretation, and as we ask God for understanding, it is the Holy Spirit that reveals the meaning to us. In my experience, that is through thoughts or words going through my mind that I wouldn't usually be thinking. For example, one time, I dreamt about a dog being strung up to be killed, then cut down off the rope and then another dog coming along to eat it. It's a pretty weird dream, right? When I prayed about what this might mean (if anything), I thought I would look up what dogs meant in the Bible. I found that a human being being eaten by a dog was the most disgraceful thing that could happen to a person (see for example 1 Kings 21:19, 23–24) and that Paul referred to legalistic people as dogs (see Philippians 3:2). The interpretation in the context I was facing was 'legalists will be cut down and disgraced.'

Dallas Willard did some brilliant work about how we know it is the indwelling Spirit we hear, not just our thoughts or perceptions. I encourage you to read his book *Hearing God*[114]. I don't intend to go into great depth about this, but to summarise from Willard, three factors are to be considered: the weight of authority in the voice, the 'spirit' of the voice and the content of the voice.

The weight refers to the impact of the impression that its communications make on our consciousness; 'There is a certain steady and calm force with which communications from God impact our soul, our innermost being, inclining us towards assent and even towards active compliance … We sense inwardly the immediate power of God's voice'[115].

The 'spirit' of the voice 'is a spirit of exalted peacefulness and confidence, of joy, of sweet reasonableness and of will for the good. It is, in short, "the spirit of Jesus", and by that I refer to the overall tone and internal dynamics of his personal life as a whole'[116].

Finally, the content of the voice, which, if truly from God, 'will always conform to, be consistent with, the truths about God's nature and kingdom that are made clear in the Bible'[117].

I would add one other way of knowing to this list, which is the fruit of our obedience to what we believe the Holy Spirit is saying. Are we growing in the 'fruits of the Spirit' such as love, joy, peace, patience, kindness, goodness, gentleness and self-control (see Galatians 5:22–26)? When we share with someone a word of encouragement that the Holy Spirit has prompted or a gentle correction, does it resonate with them? Someone once asked me, upon sharing some words of encouragement with a couple of people, how I knew it was God. I responded, 'Because I have tested this voice many times, and when I obey, things happen or people are responsive'. It takes a risk to follow those promptings, but the risk pays off nine times out of ten[118]. Jesus said that we would know false prophets from the bad fruit in their life; therefore, I conclude the inverse is also true, that we know true prophets or those who are really hearing from the Holy Spirit by the good fruit in their life (see Matthew 7:15–20). There is a caveat to this. Sometimes, there are gifted people who do hear from God but whose character is still being developed. We can't throw the baby out with the bathwater in these instances. If we did, there would be no Moses, David, Peter, etc. Sin doesn't disqualify us from hearing the voice of God, but we need to repent when we recognise sin, as these heroes of the faith did, and continue to grow more Christlike.

As alluded to, we learn to know God's voice through the Spirit by experience. Just as we learn to recognise a human friend's voice the more we spend time with them, the more we intentionally spend time with Jesus, the easier it will become to recognise His voice[119]. There is also a word of caution here, no matter how experienced we may be. Sometimes we get it wrong. We may think the Holy Spirit has said something to us only to find out that, when tested, it was off the mark. This can lead to discouragement and even an abandonment of seeking the Lord's voice for discernment for ourselves or other people. Our adversary, Satan, doesn't want us to tune in to the Spirit of Jesus and can bring all kinds of distraction and discouragement in our pursuit of this. But Jesus promises that 'my sheep hear my voice' so we can press into that promise when feeling confused.

It is also helpful to pray with others and participate in 'group discernment' to learn and grow our confidence in hearing the Spirit. We see that the prophets and teachers at Antioch did just that when setting aside Paul and Barnabas for the mission God had for them. They worshipped *together* and fasted *together*, and the Holy Spirit spoke in this context. In *Celebration of Discipline*, Richard Foster remarked, 'With all our modern methods of missionary recruitment, we could profit by giving serious attention to this example of corporate guidance. We would be well advised to encourage groups of people to fast, pray, and worship together until they have discerned the mind of the Lord'[120]. To that, I say, 'Amen'!

Paul also put a safeguard in place when it came to giving public revelation from God. He said to the church in Corinth, 'Let two or three prophets speak [as inspired by the Holy Spirit], while the rest pay attention and weigh carefully what is said' (1 Corinthians 14:29 AMP). The word 'weigh' literally means 'to separate thoroughly' and can be translated as discern, evaluate or judge. We need the body of Christ to help each other discern the voice of the Holy Spirit. If someone does get it wrong, they don't need disparaging remarks or rebuke but encouragement to continue their pursuit of God and people to come alongside them to help them grow in their discernment of the Holy Spirit's voice. As Dallas Willard said, 'God does not intend to make us infallible by his conversational walk with us'[121].

It is an absolute privilege that the Spirit of Jesus desires to dwell within those who have been born again. Do not take this for granted; instead, learn to be led by the Spirit like the early church leaders and first missionaries. There is no greater adventure.

Now, I want to change tracks and relate how God spoke to a grieving mother from Zimbabwe through an 'internal voice'.

Susan's Story — Heartbreak to hope

It was the hardest thing that I've ever had to walk through. My beautiful eleven-year-old daughter woke up feeling unwell on 28 September 2009. By 7.30 pm that night, she had gone. I was in total shock, and my heart was shattered. After that day, I was scared of God. I didn't trust Him. I continued to go to church, worship and read the Bible but kept God at a distance, at arm's length, so to speak. I had many questions, such as *does God just do things unexpectedly, and you don't know what will happen next? Is life so uncertain?*

Obviously, my heart was broken, and I couldn't fix it. I think I was just trying to bandage myself with the Word of God.

People would come around me to comfort and encourage me, to pray for me, and to do all these kinds of things, which was good and nice, but it didn't heal my broken heart.

Two years later, my husband and I joined Youth for Christ. We went to Namibia for training and, while we were there, we watched an evangelism training video called 'The Bridge Master'. It's about a man who operated a train bridge. One day, this man went to work with his son. There was a moment when he stepped out of the booth for a short amount of time. His son was by the edge of the river, by the bridge, and he noticed a train coming, but his dad hadn't let the bridge down. He knew that there was another way of opening the bridge without going into his dad's little booth. So he went to let the bridge down for the train. But as he was doing that, his dad got back into the booth and noticed the train coming with just seconds to go before the train hit the bridge.

The Bridge Master realised that if he let the bridge down at that moment, his son would get crushed. So he had a split second to decide: *do I let the bridge down and save the people on the train, or do I sacrifice the people on the train to save my son?* He's frantic, slamming his fists into the booth and in total despair, but ultimately, he chooses to sacrifice his son. Eventually, the train comes past, and different people are on the train: families, soldiers, drug addicts, and all kinds of people. (The video is used to explain how God so loved the world that He gave His only begotten Son). He picks up his son, and he's weeping over him. He's carrying the dead body of his son. Watching that man took me right back to the day our daughter passed away. And my heart was still so broken.

In the training the day before, we had been talking about God being the healer of our hearts and being the healer of our wounds. God had shown me the Scripture from Malachi that talks about the Son of Righteousness rising with healing in His wings (Malachi 4:2). We even had a ministry time, praying over each other and other people. But I wasn't prayed for. It's like I had my wounds, and I wanted to keep them hidden. I had this deep wound, and I was still trying to bandage it on my own. I felt like it was my job to fix it.

But that following day, when we watched 'The Bridge Master', it was like God ripped off my bandages, exposed that deep wound, all the grief and pain, and my shattered heart. As I sat there in my brokenness, I heard the words flashing in my mind, 'Susan, I understand what it is to lose a child.' Everything in the room seemed to go silent. I couldn't hear what was being said anymore. I sat there crying, and I had to leave the classroom. I went to my room, and there I surrendered. I cried, 'Lord, I give you my heart. Please heal my heart.' I sat there for about two hours in a place of surrender, just weeping and trusting God to do what only He could do, what no human doctor could do, what no person could do. After those two hours, I felt okay, like, 'I'm okay now.' I got up, washed my face, and returned to the classroom.

I realised that I had believed the lie that God didn't understand, that God is far away up there and that I'm down here just trying to live and just trying to get by. I felt like I'd told myself, 'Just let God be God, and I'll be me, and I'll try to handle this as best I can.' But He showed me that He *did* understand and that He wanted me to go to Him because He knew what it was like to watch His own child suffer.

When I went back to the classroom, the woman who was sitting next to me leaned over and said, 'Excuse me, Susan. God told me to tell you something, and I wrote it down.' I said, 'Oh, okay. What is it?' She handed me this piece of paper, and on it was written, 'I understand.'

God *wanted* me to ask Him to heal my heart. And He did. He doesn't override our will. It's like going to the doctor. I mean, I'll get up and go to the doctor and say, 'Oh, Doctor, please help me. I've been having a headache for five days.' And then the doctor uses his authority to prescribe the medication we need to feel better. So with God. I had been sitting with this deep wound for about two years, a broken heart that nothing or no one could fix. I needed to ask God for help and to heal my heart. Grief is a process; it's a journey. I still miss my daughter because I love her, and I always will, but it's like the grief shifted from one level to another. I had peace in my heart and knew that God had healed it. I am so thankful that God spoke to me and told me that He understood what it was like to lose a child.

HIGHLIGHT *from* HISTORY

Jackie Pullinger — Missionary and founder of St Stephen's Society

For this 'Highlight from History,' I have chosen someone who is still alive at the time of writing. However, her story of God speaking and leading by the Holy Spirit has inspired many, including myself, through her book *Chasing the Dragon*[122].

Born in London in 1944[123], Jackie grew up going to Sunday School. When she was five years old, a visiting missionary came and spoke to her class, pointing to each one and asking, 'And could God want you on the mission field?'[124] As a young girl, she would tell her friends that she would be a missionary, although she didn't understand what that meant. Fast forward a few years, and she was confirmed in the Anglican Church, which filled her with great joy. Immediately, she began looking into different missionary societies with the thought of preparing herself for the mission field. However, while she believed in God, she didn't have a personal relationship with Him and, as a young woman in her college years, loved to party and had dismissed the idea of being a missionary. While studying piano and oboe at the Royal College of Music, she was invited to a Bible study. She encountered a group of young Christians who impressed her with their 'normality' and evident love for Jesus.

Through the sharing of the gospel and the 'shock' that no one could come to God except through Jesus, she was 'constrained either to accept what Jesus had said about Himself or to forget about the Christian faith'[125]. She gave her life to Christ that night, and the missionary zeal immediately returned. She wrote to many missionary societies, schools and other agencies but was rejected by each one, yet she had the overwhelming sense that God was asking her to go and to trust Him.

God continued to speak, through a dream and then later, a vision in her mind (the imagination) in which she saw a woman beseechingly holding out her arms with the words coming across her mind like a scrolling television credit: 'WHAT CAN YOU GIVE US?'

Yet she was still being rejected by any mission agency. While helping a Vicar during one of her Easter holiday breaks, she plucked up the courage to ask him for advice about her situation. She knew God was asking her to go, but she didn't know where. 'If God is telling you to go, you had better go,' was his reply[126].

'How can I – I don't know where to. All my applications have been rejected,' Jackie stated[127].

The Vicar advised, 'If I were you, I would go out and buy a ticket for a boat going on the longest journey you can find and pray to know where to get off'[128].

This idea excited Jackie – she just had to trust God and follow wherever God led. She went out and bought the cheapest ticket with the longest route: France to Japan. So in 1966, at twenty-two years of age, she set sail without knowing her final destination. While one of the dreams suggested that Hong Kong was where God was leading her, it wasn't until she arrived in Hong Kong harbour that she knew where she should get off. With six British Pounds, no job and no connections (besides her mother's godson), she began her life as a missionary to the drug addicts and gang members of what was then the infamous 'walled city of Hong Kong'[129].

Many people miraculously got off heroin and other drugs, and she began taking people into her home. The need for housing for rehabilitation was obvious and, in 1981, the St Stephen's Society[130] was founded to house and rehabilitate addicts. It has grown far and wide in the years since, seeing thousands of people set free by the good news of the gospel and the power of the Spirit. All because one woman was willing to hear God's voice through the Spirit and was also willing to obey.

Reflect

How about you? Have you heard the whisper of the indwelling Holy Spirit prompting you to go? Perhaps it's like Jackie stepping into an unknown future with little resource or connection, or maybe it's going to the person down the street. Are you willing to say 'yes' to those promptings? Taking a step of faith is part of the adventure of following Jesus. May you have ears to hear and a heart to respond to the voice of the indwelling Spirit of Jesus.

[109] I detailed this and similar experiences in my book: Walker, Lyndal J. (2023). *Intimacy, Intercession, and Increase: An Adventure with Jesus to Explore a Life of Prayer*. YFCI, Denver, CO, p. 108.

[110] Deere, Jack. (1996). *Surprised by the Voice of God: How God Speaks Today Through Prophecies, Dreams, and Visions*. Zondervan, Grand Rapids, MI, p. 151.

[111] The Greek is 'hagiazo'. *Olive Tree Enhanced Strong's Dictionary*.

[112] Foster, R. (2008). *Celebration of Discipline: The Path to Spiritual Growth*. Hodder & Stoughton Ltd, London, p. 30.

[113] To see how to do this, go to: https://www.jesuit.org.uk/spirituality/imaginative-contemplation#:~:text=It%20is%20a%20method%20of,imagination%20as%20through%20your%20thoughts (Accessed 3 May 2024).

[114] Willard, D. (1999). *Hearing God: Building an Intimate Relationship with the Creator.* HarperCollins Religious, London.

[115] ibid. p. 169.

[116] ibid. p. 171.

[117] ibid. p. 172.

[118] I have not done any scientific research on this matter. I'm just using this as a figure of speech!

[119] For a good exploration of this see Willard, D. (1999). *Hearing God: Building an Intimate Relationship with the Creator*. HarperCollins Religious, London, pp. 160–163.

[120] Foster, R. (2008). *Celebration of Discipline: The Path to Spiritual Growth*. Hodder & Stoughton Ltd, London, p. 221.

[121] Willard, D. (1999). *Hearing God: Building an Intimate Relationship with the Creator*. HarperCollins Religious, London, p. 176.

[122] Pullinger, J. (With Andrew Quicke). (2010). *Chasing the Dragon: One woman's struggle against the darkness of Hong Kong's drug dens*, Hodder and Stoughton, London.

[123] https://en.wikipedia.org/wiki/Jackie_Pullinger (Accessed 7 May 2024).

[124] Pullinger, J. (With Andrew Quicke). (2010). Chasing the Dragon, Hodder and Stoughton, London, p. 13.

[125] ibid. p. 17.

[126] ibid. p. 21.

[127] ibid. p. 21.

[128] ibid. p. 21.

[129] I highly recommend reading *Chasing the Dragon* to get a sense of how horrific this environment was and to see how God used Jackie to reach the people living there.

[130] https://www.ststephenssociety.com/ (Accessed 9 May 2024).

"Behold, I Stand At The Door And Knock..."

A reinterpretation of The Light of the World (1851-1854) by William Holman Hunt, illustrating Revelations 3:20: "Behold, I stand at the door and knock; if any man hear my voice, and open the door, I will come into him, and will sup with him, and he with Me." In the original painting, the door is without a handle, and can only be opened from the inside. The artist had come to faith later in life, and it was discovered beneath the moulding, Hunt had written the words: "Forgive me, Lord Jesus, that I kept you waiting so long!" (William J. Bausch, *More telling Stories, Compelling Stories*, p.2).

Chapter Ten

Postscript: Your Story

As you have read the stories throughout this book, some may have resonated with you more than others. That's how it should be. We are all in a unique relationship with the God of the universe, and He will speak to us uniquely. And before you think, I *can't hear God. I've tried but don't get anything back;* if you are a Christian, you have heard God speak. That's how you came to follow Jesus in the first place[131].

Maybe, as you've read, it has triggered something in you. You have had different experiences where you thought it probably was God trying to get your attention, but you put it to the back of your mind and have just gotten on with life as you know it. There is grace to be found if that is you, and it's never too late to respond to that voice. As has been said, we get to know the voice of God through experience, and if we intentionally posture our hearts towards the One who speaks, we will begin to learn what He sounds like to us.

Is the effort worth it? The answer for me is a resounding yes. Why?

Because:

- God loves us and wants an intimate relationship with us
- It is the way to true life: free and abundant
- He wants His kingdom extended in the world

He loves us

It would be a pretty strange marriage if a husband and wife sat down at the dinner table every night, and the wife listed all the things she wanted her husband to do and then walked away. We would say that was a pretty dysfunctional marriage. Yet, that is often how we treat our relationship with the Lamb of God (2 Corinthians 11:2, Revelation 19:7–9). We come to Him with all our requests and what we would like Him to do for us, which is good and right, yet there is so much more to prayer than simply asking. God loved us so much that He sent His only son so that no one would perish but have eternal life (John 3:16). Jesus defines what eternal life is in John 17:3, 'And this is eternal life, that they *know* [my emphasis] you, the only true God, and Jesus Christ whom you have sent.' That word for 'know' in the original Greek is the word *ginosko* and means 'to learn to know, come to know, get a knowledge of, perceive, feel'[132]. This word was even used as a Jewish idiom for sexual intimacy between a man and a woman[133]. Isn't it amazing that we can get to know the God of the universe in such a uniquely personal way, not just with a head knowledge, but a deeply personal, loving knowledge? We can learn what He thinks about us, what His plans are for us, and what His desires for this world are. In other words, we can have a conversation with God.

But to know Him this way, we need to know what His voice sounds like. Jesus said to the church in Laodicea, people who were neither hot nor cold in their works with Him (therefore pretty useless[134]) and who were living in self-sufficiency because of their wealth, 'Here I am! I stand at the door and knock. If anyone hears my voice and opens the door, I will come in and eat with that person, and they with me' (Revelation 3:20 NIV). Often, we hear this verse used in the context of people who don't know Jesus as an invitation to them to respond to His call for salvation, but Jesus spoke these words to people who *already* knew Him. Sadly, they had kept Him out of their inner sanctum. To eat and drink with another person in the ancient world was an act of honour and acceptance and a sign of intimate friendship between those dining[135]. This is the invitation He is offering us. He wants to come and sit around the table with us, even to the point of John's intimacy when He was able to recline with Him (John 13:23). But He doesn't just want to come in for a one-off meal; He wants to make His home in us (Ephesians 3:17–19). The same invitation Jesus gave to the Laodiceans He gives to you today. Will you give up your useless deeds, repent from your self-sufficiency, open the door and let Him in? The fellowship offered is rich and rewarding, and from it flows the works that will produce fruit with an eternal reward, the fruit that is dependent on His sufficiency and not our own, for 'apart from me you can do nothing' (John 15:5).

He wants us to live a free and abundant life

Jesus said that He came to give life and life in abundance (John 10:10). That means an absolute fullness of life, active and vigorous, over and beyond what we can imagine[136]. To have that kind of life, we must be free from the bondage of sin, for the wages of sin is death (Romans 6:23). Sin means 'to miss the mark' or to do something wrong according to God's divine law[137]. This manifests in selfishness and pride, wanting to live according to our desires instead of God's. Living this way may feel good in the moment, but it leads to misery and eternal judgment (Romans 2:3–11). Jesus dealt with sin at the cross so that we could be cleansed of sin and free from that bondage, but often, sin's deceptive ways (Hebrews 3:13) can lead us astray little by little until we are at the point where we wonder how we even got there (see James 1:13–15). As we converse with Jesus, the Good Shepherd who wants to protect His sheep (John 10:11), He makes us aware of our selfishness and brings us back to the path of righteousness (Psalm 23:3).

Richard Foster says,

> Inward fellowship of this kind transforms the inner personality. We cannot burn the eternal flame of the inner sanctuary and remain the same, for the Divine Fire will consume everything that is impure. Our ever-present Teacher will always be leading us into 'righteousness and peace and joy in the Holy Spirit' (Romans 14:17). Everything

that is foreign to his way we will have to let go. No, not 'have to' but 'want to', for our desires and aspirations will be more and more conformed to his way. Increasingly, everything within us will swing like a needle to the polestar of the Spirit[138].

If you have confessed your sin to Jesus, you are forgiven! You can't be condemned anymore if you are in Christ Jesus, for God condemned sin already when Jesus hung on the cross (Romans 8:1–3)[139]. Therefore, when we struggle with sin, we can boldly come to Jesus and ask for help (Hebrews 4:14–16). Jesus will converse with us to help us overcome our temptations and give us the assurance and comfort we need. He may lead us to share our struggles with someone else (James 5:16) or give us other guidance to live the victorious over-sin, abundant life that He intends for us. Don't be afraid to go to God with your struggles. He knows and cares (1 Peter 5:6–7).

I love what Dallas Willard said in his book *Hearing God*,

Oh, we can 'get by' with a God who does not speak. Many at least think they do. But it is not much of a life, and certainly not the life intended for us by God or the abundance of life that Jesus Christ came to make available. Without real communication from God, our view of the world is very impersonal, however glorious we may find God's creation[140].

So get out there, start listening to the sound of God for yourself, and live the life He always intended for you!

He wants His kingdom to spread in this world

The third compelling reason it's worth pressing into hearing God's voice is that He wants partners in His mission of reaching the lost. As Paul says in 1 Corinthians 3:9, those who serve Christ are God's fellow workers. The original Greek word for 'fellow workers' is *synergos*, from '*syn*' denoting union with or together[141] and 'ergon' – toil, deed, work, labour[142]. Does that remind you of an English word? The English word 'synergy' comes from this Greek word and means 'the interaction or cooperation of two or more organisations, substances, or other agents *to produce a combined effect greater than the sum of their separate effects* [my emphasis]'[143].

Isn't that amazing? God's intention is to partner with humans in spreading the good news of the kingdom of God. He poured out the Holy Spirit at Pentecost so the disciples could have the power to be Jesus's witnesses to the local area, then the region, and even to the ends of the earth (Acts 1:8). Jesus told them before He departed to go and make disciples of all nations … and that He would always be with them (Matthew 28:16–20).

We don't just need God's power to be His witnesses, but we need His direction, and we get that through being with Him and hearing His voice. We have already discovered how Paul was directed by the voice of the Holy Spirit in the mission God gave Him. If we are serious about our call to mission, we must learn to hear God's voice as we go. It could be as simple as posing the question, 'Jesus, who would you want me to talk to about you this week?' to hearing from Him for a strategic plan to reach a whole region, but whatever we are doing in co-labouring with Him, it begins with Him speaking to us. This makes mission an exciting prospect, not something we do out of obligation or a job title. It also means that we are open to being 'interrupted' by His voice when we need to change tracks or even stop doing something we might have been doing for a long time. Ultimately, it's about how He wants to achieve His mission through us. I hope the thought of this reinvigorates you for the journey ahead.

So where are you at?

By now, I hope you have realised that the purpose of this book isn't for you just to read some nice stories and be uplifted (although that's great in and of itself). I hope that by hearing these stories and understanding the different ways God speaks, you will have a greater hunger to know and experience Him for yourself. You don't have to leave these stories on the pages of a book – you can enter these stories yourself as you humble yourself before the Almighty God and ask Him to speak. If you are hungry for more, there are many excellent resources for further discovery, such as those mentioned in the footnotes. Or ask someone more experienced in this area to mentor you.

Knowing God and hearing from Him is the most exciting adventure. There will be plenty of challenges along the way, but you will always have Someone who walks with you through these challenges. If you have yet to come into a personal relationship with this amazing God, you can pray a simple prayer to begin the journey:

> *God, I recognise that I have chosen the way of sin, which has separated me from you. I confess that you are God, that you sent Jesus to this world to die for my sins and the sins of this world and that He was raised after three days. I ask you to forgive me for my sin, cleanse and make me new. I invite you to come and make your home in me. I completely surrender to you. Teach me to know your voice and to walk with you. Thank you for saving me.*

If you have just sincerely prayed this prayer, welcome to the family! You are not alone; people are waiting to welcome you into the community. Contact a local church or Youth for Christ Centre in your area. We need each other to live life as God intended.

When it is all said and done, when our life on earth is over, the only thing we will take with us into eternity is our relationship with God. So, isn't it worth investing in that relationship now? You can begin *your* story of hearing the sound of God today.

131 Wilson, A. (2014). 'How do we hear God?': https://www.premierchristianity.com/home/how-do-we-hear-god/2911 (Accessed 4 June 2024).

132 *Olive Tree Enhanced Strong's Dictionary*, g1097.

133 ibid.

134 Weima, J. A. D. (2021). *The Sermons to the Seven Churches of Revelation*. Baker Academic, Grand Rapids, Michigan, p. 239.

135 Weima, J. A. D. (2021). T*he Sermons to the Seven Churches of Revelation*. Baker Academic, Grand Rapids, Michigan, p. 255–256.

136 *Olive Tree Enhanced Strong's Dictionary*, g2222, g4053.

137 *Olive Tree Enhanced Strong's Dictionary*, g0266.

138 Foster, R. (2008). *Celebration of Discipline: The Path to Spiritual Growth*. Hodder & Stoughton Ltd, London, p. 24.

139 However, read all of Romans 8 to understand the freedom from sin available to us.

140 Willard, D. (1999). *Hearing God: Building an Intimate Relationship with the Creator*. HarperCollins Religious, London, p. 180.

141 *Olive Tree Enhanced Strong's Dictionary*, g4862.

142 *Olive Tree Enhanced Strong's Dictionary*, g2041.

143 From Oxford Languages, accessed by Google Search on July 2, 2024.

Want to read more stories?

Scan the QR code (yfci.org/god-has-a-sound-by-lyndal-j-walker) to read more amazing stories of YFC workers from around the globe hearing *The Sound of God*.

To find out about the work of YFC go to **yfci.org**.

Acknowledgements

Thank you to all the YFC workers who allowed me to tell their stories in this book. You are wonderful, and your obedience is producing a lot of fruit.

I'm so grateful for the support of my boss, Chris Kozacek. He lets me be free to follow the voice of the Lord. I also want to thank Dave and Katy Brereton for championing prayer in our organisation.

Thanks to Lynne, Katy and Susan, who pray for me every week and especially for praying for this project, as well as the rest of my prayer supporters!

Thanks to those who have 'sown' into this project to allow it to be published. Your financial support is such a blessing.

Thanks to the amazingly talented Kylie Inglis, who provided the artwork and acted as a sounding board throughout this project.

Thank you to Warwick Vincent and Karen Bott for reading my draft and providing invaluable feedback. I also want to thank Caleb Bowles for reading and giving feedback on chapter 9.

Thank you to Leysa for your beautiful design work and patience throughout the process!

Thanks, Adam, for writing the foreword and faithfully obeying God's voice in your life.

Thanks to my family and other supporters who continue giving in many ways.

About the author

Lyndal J. Walker is on a mission to help people hear God's voice and grow in their faith. As the prayer director for Youth for Christ International (and previously the prayer coordinator for Youth for Christ Australia), she spends her days equipping others to deepen their relationship with God—one prayer at a time.

In 2021, she released her first book, *Intimacy, Intercession and Increase: An adventure with Jesus* to explore a life of prayer, a devotional designed to make prayer an exciting, everyday adventure. Her latest book explores the many ways God speaks, because she firmly believes that hearing from Him isn't just for the 'spiritually elite'—it's for everyone!

When she's not writing, ministering, or praying up a storm, you'll probably find Lyndal keeping fit, cheering on professional tennis players, or planning her next travel adventure. She's based in Melbourne, Australia, but let's be honest—she's rarely in one place for long!

To find out more about Lyndal and her work go to **lyndaljwalker.com**

www.ingramcontent.com/pod-product-compliance
Lightning Source LLC
Chambersburg PA
CBHW041808160426
43209CB00028B/1899/J